EX LIBRIS

CHERISHED

LIBRARY
BOOK HOUSE

Gabriel N Cherish

Kings & Queens

A Very Peculiar History™

With added blue blood

'To be a king and wear a crown is a thing more glorious to them that see it than it is pleasant to them that bear it.'

Queen Elizabeth I, 1601

To my wife, Myriam, a treasured source of wise counsel, like her compatriot Philippa of Hainault, who persuaded her husband Edward III to spare the Burghers of Calais in 1347.

AM

Editors: Victoria England, Jamie Pitman

Artists: David Antram, Mark Bergin, Ray and Corinne Burrows, Simon Calder, Carolyn Franklin, John James, Mark Peppé

Published by **S**SCRIBO
25 Marlborough Place, Brighton BN1 1UB
A division of Book House, an imprint of
The Salariya Book Company Ltd.

ISBN 978-1-4351-5989-1

Printed and bound in China.
Printed on paper from
sustainable sources.

1 3 5 7 9 8 6 4 2

Kings & Queens

A Very Peculiar History™

With added blue blood

Written by
Antony Mason

Created and designed by
David Salariya

 SCRIBO

The British National Anthem

God save our gracious Queen,
Long live our noble Queen,
God save the Queen:
Send her victorious,
Happy and glorious,
Long to reign over us:
God save the Queen.

O Lord, our God, arise,
Scatter her enemies,
And make them fall.
Confound their politics,
Frustrate their knavish tricks,
On Thee our hopes we fix,
God save us all.

Thy choicest gifts in store,
On her be pleased to pour;
Long may she reign:
May she defend our laws,
And ever give us cause
To sing with heart and voice
God save the Queen.

Contents

Ten peculiar royal facts

The British royal family has always been a bit of a mixed bag. Members of the family have been, or could be said to be:

1. **Foreign:** After the Normans, for over 300 years the kings of England spoke French as their first language. Henry V (1413–1422) may have been the first king to speak English with ease. The Hanoverian kings, starting with George I, spoke German. Even Queen Victoria used German at home, and never learnt to speak English perfectly.

2. **Jumpy:** During William the Conqueror's coronation at Westminster Abbey, his guards massacred a crowd of Anglo-Saxon supporters: they mistook their cheers for a rebellion.

3. **Spooky:** The ghost of Catherine Howard, the executed fifth wife of Henry VIII, is said to haunt Hampton Court Palace, and is responsible for the name of the 'Haunted Gallery' there.

4. **Suspect:** When James II's second wife gave birth to a son, there was suspicion that she was too old, and that someone else's baby had been smuggled into the room in a warming pan. Thereafter, until the mid-20th century (up to the birth of Princess Margaret in

1930), all royal births had to be witnessed by the Home Secretary, a government minister.

5. **Learned:** King James I (VI of Scotland) wrote books on witchcraft, the dangers of tobacco and the duties of kingship.

6. **Gross:** Queen Anne had grown so large by the time of her death (swollen by body fluids from the condition called dropsy, now known as oedema) that she had to be buried in a coffin that was almost square.

7. **Unlucky:** William III died after his horse stumbled over a molehill in 1714. After this, supporters of the rival Stuart dynasty would raise a toast to the 'velvet-coated gentleman' (the mole).

8. **Lucky:** Queen Victoria survived seven assassination attempts.

9. **Measured:** The old imperial measurement, the yard, was said to be based on the distance between Henry I's nose and his outstretched fingertip.

10. **Well connected:** Queen Elizabeth II can trace her ancestry back over 1,000 years to Alfred the Great, the first King of England, who ruled from AD 871 to 899.

Putting royalty on the map

Some famous and important royal
residences and battlegrounds.

✗ = SITE OF
BATTLE

SCOTLAND

Battle of Stirling
Bridge

NORTHERN
IRELAND

Battle of
the Boyne

IRELAND

ENGLAND

Battle of
Bosworth Field

WALES

Battle of Hastings

1. Buckingham Palace, London
2. Balmoral Castle, Scotland
3. Sandringham House, Norfolk
4. Palace of Holyroodhouse, Edinburgh
5. Castle of Mey, Scotland
6. Windsor Castle, Berkshire
7. Osborne House, Isle of Wight
8. Brighton Pavilion, East Sussex
9. Kew Palace, London
10. Winchester, Saxon capital of Wessex
11. Scone, first capital of Scotland
12. Canterbury Cathedral, Kent
13. Sherwood Forest, Nottinghamshire
14. Berkeley Castle, Gloucestershire
15. Oxford Castle, Oxfordshire

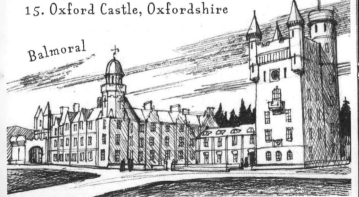

Balmoral

The elements of the **Royal Coat of Arms** have been gradually put together since the time of Richard I 'The Lionheart' in the 12th century. The symbols on the shield show the three lions of England, the lion of Scotland and the harp of Ireland. The 'supporters' are a lion (for England) and a unicorn (for Scotland).

'*Honi soit qui mal y pense*' ('*Shame be to him who thinks evil of it*') is the motto of the Order of the Garter: tradition holds that Edward III said this when gallantly picking up a lady's fallen garter at a dance.

'*Dieu et mon droit*' ('*God and my right*') refers to the divine or God-given right of the monarch to govern.

INTRODUCTION

Britain is still ruled by a Queen. Well, 'ruled' may not be quite the right word, but she is Head of State, and she still has a considerable amount of influence over the way Britain is run. Some 1,200 years ago, when our story begins, kings had the power to do just about anything they liked. They were nice only if they wanted to be, but generally got their way through force, general bullying, and perhaps murder and mayhem – if no-one murdered them first.

Over those 1,200 years the power of the kings and queens of Britain has been gradually whittled away. Today, Britain is governed primarily by Parliament, and the people have a choice about who governs them, which they exercise through elections. It took centuries of struggle to reach this point, because the kings and queens were not going to give up their powers voluntarily. One – Charles I – was so obstinate he ended up having his head chopped off.

So, we can vote for our government. But nobody votes for the monarch. Instead, the hereditary principle controls who will be the next king or queen. It's usually the eldest son of the current king or queen; if there is no son, it is the eldest daughter. Not very democratic, you might say. But it is, in that British citizens, in general, accept this as the way things are done. It has been done like this for hundreds of years, and they don't want to change it. There are plenty of people who wonder if this is fair or right: republicans argue that the whole idea of monarchy is wrong. But then you ask who you would want instead as a Head of State. Another elected politician as a President? Arguments about getting rid of the monarchy usually end there. There is just is no alternative that is as good.

The Queen provides continuity. Other, elected rulers come and go. Since she has been on the throne, a dozen Prime Ministers have passed through her doors. She is able to advise her ministers using the benefits of over 50 years of experience. Because she has reigned so long, she is also probably one of the best-known and most respected heads in the world today. That's quite an advantage on the world stage.

It is a role that is deeply embedded in history, and is surrounded by age-old ceremony, ritual and pageant. These are important symbols of British identity, and powerful stimulants for feelings of national pride.

Yet Britons still feel they have a choice. The Queen rules with their permission. If ever a deeply unpopular king or queen inherited the throne, the monarchy might come to an end there and then, and 1,200 years of history would be tossed out of the window. This might not be entirely unwelcome to members of the royal family themselves. Would you want the job?

Queen Boudicca

A famous symbol of British resistance to foreign invasion, Boudicca (or Boadicea to the Romans), was a warrior queen in the early days of Roman occupation. Her husband was the king of the Iceni tribe of Norfolk. When he died, the Romans tried to annex the Iceni lands, stirring up a revolt led by Boudicca. Her forces sacked Roman settlements in Colchester, St Albans and London, wiped out the 9th Legion and killed some 70,000 Romans before Boudicca was captured. She committed suicide rather than be taken to Rome in chains.

King Arthur

The stories of King Arthur and the Knights of the Round Table form a magnificent set of folk tales centring on his legendary castle of Camelot. Where was Camelot? Some say the West Country of England, which was under attack from Saxon invaders in the 6th century AD; some say Brittany. Some claim he was King of the Britons, in southern Scotland, and that his capital was Edinburgh – hence the mountain in Edinburgh is still known as Arthur's Seat. All these are Celtic regions. The stories are probably only vaguely linked to historical fact – but they gained currency in medieval times, as idealised visions of kingship and knightly honour and valour.

How it all began

Histories of the kings and queens of Britain usually begin in the 8th century AD. But there had been kings and queens before that. When the Romans conquered Britain in AD 43, they found a patchwork of local tribes, ruling their territories from hill forts. They had their leaders, who might be described as kings and queens. The Romans, with their technically advanced weapons, found them easy enough to conquer, and they went on to rule Britain for four centuries, under the control of a succession of governors appointed by the Emperor in Rome.

The word 'king' comes from the Old English *cyning*, related to Old German *kunig* and Old Danish *konge*. 'Queen' comes from Old English *cwēn*, meaning simply 'wife'. That tells us about the origins of the tradition: they date back to the time after the Romans left Britain (in around AD 450), when tribes of invaders and settlers entered Britain – tribes such as the Angles and Saxons from Germany, and later the Norse Vikings from Scandinavia. Our story begins with the Saxons.

List of Saxon kings
802–1016*

Egbert, 802–839: King of Wessex
Ethelwulf, 839–858: son of Egbert
Ethelbald, 858–860: son of Ethelwulf
Ethelbert, 860–865/6: son of Ethelwulf
Ethelred I, 865/6–871: son of Ethelwulf
Alfred the Great, 871–899: son of Ethelwulf
Edward 'The Elder', 899–924/5: son of
  Alfred
Alfward, 924–?: son of Edward the Elder
Athelstan 'The Glorious', 925–939: son of
  Edward the Elder
Edmund I 'The Magnificent', 939–946: son
  of Edward the Elder
Eadred, 946–955: son of Edward the Elder
Eadwig 'The Fair', 955–959: son of Edmund I
Edgar 'The Peaceful', 959–975: son of
  Edmund I
Edward 'The Martyr', 975–978: son of Edgar
Ethelred II 'Unraed', 978–1016: son of Edgar
Edmund II 'Ironside', 1016: son of Ethelred
  II 'Unraed'

---

* *The dates given are dates of reigns, not birth and death dates.*

CHAPTER ONE

THE SAXONS

I n the 8th century, some three hundred years after the Romans left Britain, England was ruled as a collection of kingdoms. The three largest were Northumbria in the north; Mercia in the middle; and Wessex in the south. The southeast was divided into East Anglia, Essex, Kent and Sussex.

From AD 793, the Vikings began to arrive from Scandinavia, raiding and pillaging – but also settling, especially in the north. The kingdoms of England needed to join forces to face this threat. It was the Saxon kings of Wessex who achieved this. Their capital was Winchester.

The Angles and the Saxons had come from a northern part of Germany, and settled in the southern part of Britain from the late 5th century. Egbert (reigned 802–839) founded the Saxon dynasty that ruled a territory called Wessex ('Land of the West Saxons'). He was succeeded by his son, Ethelwulf (839–858), who had five sons. Three of them, each called Ethel-something, ruled Wessex in quick succession. All the while their younger brother Alfred was learning the art of war and kingship, and in 871 it was his turn to become king.

Alfred the Great: 871–899
By this time, England was under dire threat from raiding Vikings. Alfred managed to persuade the other kingdoms – even Viking settlers in the North – to accept his leadership, so he became, effectively, the first King of 'Anglecynn' or England (a word derived from the Angles, or Anglo-Saxons). Alfred has been celebrated in legend for his wisdom, learning and sense of fair play, guided by Christian principles. He died aged about 50, and was buried in Winchester.

Alfred the Great burns the cakes!

According to legend, when Alfred was travelling in disguise to evade the Vikings, he took refuge in a simple cottage. The wife left him in charge of some cakes that were baking on the fire. But Alfred fell so deep in thought about his campaigns that he forgot about the cakes, and they burned. The wife was furious, and kicked him out of the house. Just then her husband came home and recognised Alfred. He and his wife grovelled with apologies, but Alfred reassured them, and apologised in turn for letting the cakes burn – a testament to his humility and sense of justice.

Alfred the Great's united kingdom was maintained by a series of successors, some of whom were equally great, some of whom were decidedly dodgy. In brief:

- Edward 'The Elder' (899–924/5), Alfred's son, kept the country united and stable.

- His son Alfward reigned for just two weeks or so, before dying in mysterious circumstances; or did he reign at all? The records are not clear.

- His older half-brother Athelstan (925–939) took over; did he have something to do with Alfward's death? A warrior king, he was called 'The Glorious': he triumphed over the Scots at the Battle of Brunanburh in 937, so claimed to be the First King of All Britain (conveniently forgetting Wales). But he had no children...

- ...so he was succeeded by his half-brother Edmund I (939–946), known as 'The Magnificent' for his campaigns against the Vikings. But he was stabbed to death when he personally tried to evict an outlaw who had gatecrashed his feast.

- Next came his brother, Eadred (946–955), who suffered from a mysterious digestive disorder that made him suck on his food and spit it out – a famously disgusting spectacle. Not surprisingly, perhaps, he died childless.

- He was followed by 13-year-old Eadwig (or Edwy) 'The Fair' (955–959), son of Edmund I. He died three years later.

- He was succeeded by his brother Edgar 'The Peaceful' (959–975), who managed to make Winchester a centre of art and Christian scholarship, admired across Europe. But not for long...

On his death, Edgar was succeeded by his 14-year-old son, **Edward** (975–978). But Edgar's chosen heir had actually been Edward's younger half-brother Ethelred. The country was divided, on the brink of civil war, when Edward went to stay with his stepmother. Here, aged 15, he was murdered. He became known as Edward 'The Martyr', and he was revered as a saint after miracles were attributed to his remains. He was succeeded by **Ethelred II** (978–1016). His nickname 'Unraed' meant 'Bad Advice', but he has gone down in history as 'The Unready'. Both were true: he was incompetent and badly advised, and he died after a reign of 38 years, leaving England impoverished and defenceless against the wrath of the Vikings.

The kingdom divided

Ethelred was succeeded by his son **Edmund II**, called 'Ironside' because of his tough approach to the Vikings. But before a year was up, he was roundly defeated at the Battle of Ashingdon in Essex. The Vikings made him share his kingdom with their own chosen king, **Canute**. A few weeks later Edmund was dead, assassinated in London in circumstances that remain a mystery. Canute now became King of England.

List of Viking and Saxon kings
1016–1066

VIKINGS

Canute, 1016–1035: son of Sweyn Forkbeard,
  King of Denmark
Harold I 'Harefoot' 1035–1040: son of Canute
Hardicanute, 1040–1042: son of Canute

SAXONS

Edward 'The Confessor', 1042–1066
Harold II, 1066: Brother-in-law of Edward
  the Confessor

CHAPTER TWO

THE VIKINGS

The Vikings had been causing trouble around the coasts of England, and indeed all over Europe, since the late 8th century, sailing in their longships from their homelands in Norway, Sweden and Denmark. But by the 9th century they had settled permanently in much of Britain, particularly in the North. The Viking royal families held power over kingdoms in Scandinavia as well as England. When Canute (or Cnut) took control of England, aged just 21, he was the first to break the line of Saxon kings of England, who had ruled over England for almost 150 years.

Turning back the tide

Canute was surrounded by nobles who liked to flatter him with praise. But he knew only too well the difficulties of running three kingdoms – England, Denmark and Norway – at the same time. A legend relates that one of his nobles told Canute that he was powerful enough to command even the tides. So Canute had his throne placed on the beach and sat on it until his feet got wet – to demonstrate that he was only human after all.

Peace and disorder

Canute (reigned 1016–1035) ruled with wisdom and skill. He had married Elgiva (or Aelgifu) of Northampton and had two sons with her, Sweyn and Harold 'Harefoot'. But after his conquest of England in 1016, he married Emma of Normandy, widow of Ethelred Unraed, and they had a son called Hardicanute (or Harthacnut). Canute declared that Hardicanute would be his successor. But when Canute died, Hardicanute was in Denmark, so Harold

'Harefoot' stepped in, as **Harold I** (1035–1040). When Hardicanute invaded England to claim the throne, Harold I conveniently died. So **Hardicanute** (1040–1042) took over, but he died after two years, in a drinking bout at a wedding.

Edward the Confessor

Edward was the son of Ethelred II Unraed and Emma of Normandy, so from the Saxon House of Wessex, but also half-Norman. As half-brother of Hardicanute, he became king in 1042, but he struggled to control his barons, notably his father-in-law Godwin, Earl of Wessex, and Godwin's son Harold Godwinson. Edward was deeply pious, and was said to be able to perform miracles; after his death he was made a saint and named 'The Confessor'. Apparently, he had promised the throne of England to his cousin William, Duke of Normandy. Unfortunately Harold Godwinson thought that he had promised it to him.

Chaos

When Edward the Confessor died childless in 1066, Harold Godwinson declared himself king, as **Harold II**. However, there were not just one but two rival claimants, both foreign: William, Duke of Normandy, who had the Pope's backing, and Harold Hardrada, the Viking King of Norway, who claimed that Hardicanute had promised the throne to him.

Hardrada, supported by Harold II's treacherous brother Tostig, arrived first in northern England in September 1066. Harold II raced north and won a famous victory at the Battle of Stamford Bridge on 25 September, at which Hardrada and Tostig were both killed.

Just three days later the Duke of Normandy brought a fleet of 700 ships to Pevensey on the south coast of England, where he landed unopposed. Harold II had to make a snap decision: either wait to rebuild his army, or rush south again to launch a surprise attack. He chose the latter – a decision that was to change the course of English history.

The Norman connection

The Vikings had also settled in Northern France, in an area called Normandy – a name connected to another word for Vikings: 'Norsemen'. William was the illegitimate and only son of Duke Robert I of Normandy and his mistress Arlette of Falaise. His father died when he was seven. When William took power at the age of 15, he quickly learnt to use brutal force to preserve it against rebels. He was the grandnephew of Emma of Normandy, wife of Ethelred II Unraed (and also of Canute). William claimed that their son, Edward the Confessor, had promised him the throne of England – and that Harold Godwinson had agreed.

The Battle of Hastings

Harold II's army was exhausted. They had marched 250 miles (400 km) south from Stamford Bridge. The battle began at dawn on 14 October 1066 and was bitterly fought. The armies were of about equal size – somewhere between 3,000 and 7,000 men each. Fighting raged until the evening, with the English shields, spears and axes pitted against Norman archers and knights on horseback.

William was unseated from his horse at one point. To reassure his men that he was not dead, he ripped off his helmet and shouted: 'See, I am here, I am still living and by God's help shall yet have the victory.'

In the fading light, the Normans at one point pretended to retreat; the English, scenting victory, swarmed forward, but the Normans then turned and cut them down. Harold II was killed, and for the English the battle was lost.

The events were recorded in words and pictures in the Bayeux Tapestry – a piece of embroidered cloth 68 metres (223 ft) long and 50 cm (1 ft 8 in) tall, which reads like a comic strip. It suggests that Harold was killed when he received an arrow in the eye, but that may not be the case.

After his victory, Duke William of Normandy headed for London to claim the throne of England.

English

Normans

A scene from the Battle of Hastings in the Bayeux Tapestry

List of Scottish kings
843–1058

HOUSE OF ALPIN (843–1034)

Kenneth I, 843–860: first King of Alba
Donald I, 860–862: brother of Kenneth I
Constantine I, 862–877: son of Kenneth I
Aed, 877–878: son of Kenneth I
Giric, 878–889: son of Donald I
Eochaid, 878–889 (possible joint king with Giric): grandson of Kenneth I in the female line
Donald II, 889–900: son of Constantine I
Constantine II, 900–943: son of Aed
Malcolm I, 943–954: son of Donald II
Indulf, 954–962: son of Constantine II
Dubh, 962–967: son of Malcolm I
Culen, 967–971: son of Indulf
Kenneth II, 971–995: brother of Dubh
Constantine III, 995–997: son of Culen
Kenneth III, 997–1005: son of Dubh
Malcolm II, 1005–1034: son of Kenneth II

HOUSE OF DUNKELD (1034–1058)

Duncan I, 1034–1040: grandson of Malcolm II in female line
Macbeth, 1040–1057: grandson of Malcolm II
Lulach, 1057–1058: stepson of Macbeth

CHAPTER THREE

MEANWHILE, IN SCOTLAND...

The Vikings were also attacking Scotland, a land occupied by four rival, warring kingdoms: the Picts in the north, the Scots in the west, and the Britons and Angles in the south. It was Kenneth MacAlpin (or Cinéad Mac Ailpín) who, in 843, united the Picts and Scots to face down their foes. As his name tells us, Kenneth was the son (*mac*) of Alpin, who was King of the Dál Riata Scots, a people who lived both in western Scotland and just across the sea in the north of Ireland. Scotland remained divided and fractious – and it wasn't called Scotland for another 500 years.

The Vikings targeted Christian monasteries and settlements – lured by the hope of finding church treasures. Their very first raid on the British Isles, in AD 793, struck the precious monastery of Lindisfarne, in the kingdom of the Angles. In the following years the Vikings repeatedly raided the northern coasts. Uniting the northern kingdoms was no easy task. Kenneth MacAlpin was from Dál Riata; his mother was a Pictish princess, giving him claim over Pictish lands – but it still took him five years of fighting to win them over. He made his capital in Pictland, at Scone (pronounced Skoon), near Perth. It was a

Tanistry

Kenneth MacAlpin adopted a Scottish system of succession called *tanistry*. The heir to the throne was chosen by election while the old king was still alive. The system lasted for nearly 200 years, until the death of Malcolm II, the last king of the House of Alpin. Thereafter, Scottish kings inherited the throne by direct descent, through the male line, although tanistry was the basis of a number of claims to the throne after this, such as those of Macbeth and Donald III.

rough place in a rough time: after Kenneth, a series of five kings all came to sticky ends in just 40 years:

- Donald I (860–862): allegedly murdered
- Constantine I (862–877): killed by Vikings
- Aed (877–878): murdered by his cousin and rival, Giric
- Giric (878–889): probably murdered
- Donald II (889–900): poisoned

The next king, Constantine II (900–943), ruled longer than his six predecessors; what's more, he wasn't killed, but abdicated in AD 943 to become a monk. It was Constantine II who gave his country a new name: Alba, a Gaelic word meaning something like 'Mountain Land'. But history then returned to its old pattern: seven kings in 60 years or so, all meeting violent deaths:

- Malcolm I (943–954): killed in battle
- Indulf (954–962): ditto
- Dubh (962–967): ditto
- Culen (967–971): ditto
- Kenneth II (971–995): murdered
- Constantine III (995–997): ditto
- Kenneth III (997–1005): ditto

Celtic, Gaelic, English and Scots

The Scots, Picts and Britons all spoke different forms of Celtic. Kenneth MacAlpin spoke the form of Celtic used in Dál Riata: Gaelic. After the Scots and the Picts united, Gaelic began to predominate, and Pictish faded away. The Angles spoke Anglo-Saxon, an early form of English. From around the 12th century, the English spoken in these parts developed its own distinctive form: today it is called Scots. A new word for Alba gradually emerged, used above all by the English: Scotland.

Malcolm II (1005–1034) came next and ruled for 29 years. He was nicknamed 'The Destroyer' for good reason. He defeated the Vikings, then the Northumbrians at Carham in 1018, to add Northumbria to his kingdom. He won control of the British kingdom of Strathclyde by placing his grandson Duncan on the throne. He then murdered the grandson of Kenneth III, paving the way for Duncan to inherit power over all Scotland. Malcolm II died from a hunting accident at Glamis Castle – or was it murder?

Duncan I (1034–1040) was the first king of all Scotland. He was the grandson of Malcolm II, and from the Dunkeld dynasty. Duncan wanted to pass the inheritance to his own sons, Malcolm Canmore and Donald Bane, but his cousin Macbeth claimed to be the true heir by the system of tanistry. The matter was resolved by battle near Elgin in 1040, where Duncan was killed.

Macbeth then ruled for 17 years (1040–1057). His wife Gruoch had previously been married to the King of Moray, and had a son by him called Lulach, who became Macbeth's heir. Malcolm Canmore defeated Macbeth at the Battle of Lumphanan in 1057, when Macbeth was killed. **Lulach** 'The Fool' (1057–1058) then came to the throne for only a few months before he clashed with Canmore at the Battle of Strathbogie and was killed.

In Shakespeare's play *Macbeth*, the Scottish king is portrayed as a weak man, and a murderer, manipulated by his evil wife. In reality, Macbeth was an unusually successful Scottish king, who brought relative peace to his lands.

List of Norman kings and queens
1066–1154

William I 'The Conqueror', 1066–1087
William II 'Rufus', 1087–1100: son of
  William I
Henry I, 1100–1135: son of William I
Stephen, 1135–1154: grandson of William I
Matilda, 1141: daughter of Henry I

Battle of Hastings, 1066

THE NORMANS

So, after the Battle of Hastings, William, Duke of Normandy, became King of England, the first of the Norman kings. He put his barons in charge of various parts of England, and they stamped their authority on the land. They introduced a feudal system of class-hierarchies, in which people served their lord in return for protection. William brought stonemasons with him from France, and they began building impressive fortresses and churches in cut stone blocks, with large semicircular arches. The language at court was French.

William I, the Conqueror: 1066–1087

William the Conqueror was crowned in Westminster Abbey, in London, on Christmas Day in 1066 – and this has been the place of coronation for the kings and queens of England ever since. The English were not happy to be ruled by a foreign king, but William and his barons suppressed any revolt with savage brutality. In fact, William spent most of his reign in France, waging war against the French king; he visited England just four times after 1072. While laying siege to a town near Paris, he was fatally injured when his horse stumbled. He was buried in France.

The Domesday Book

William I conducted a massive survey of England, counting who lived where, and what they owned. The main purpose was to work out how much tax everyone should pay – not a very popular concept then, as now. All the details were recorded in a book, which became known as the Domesday Book, because paying taxes was like the Day of Doom, or the Day of Reckoning at the end of the world.

William II 'Rufus': 1087–1100

William I's second son was called Rufus (= 'red') because of his ruddy complexion; according to William of Malmesbury, he also had yellow hair and was physically very strong. Ruthless and greedy, he spent much of his reign in Normandy, trying to wrest the Duchy from his older brother, Robert. When in London, he lived in the Palace of Westminster built for Edward the Confessor, and he built the magnificent Westminster Hall next door (the only original part to survive the fire of 1834).

foul play?

Hunting was a particular passion of the Norman kings, and William the Conqueror set aside vast tracts of land as royal hunting forests. William Rufus was hunting in the New Forest (in Hampshire) on 2 August 1100, when he was killed by an arrow. It was said to have been an accident. The man who supposedly fired the shot, Walter Tirel, fled abroad, but his family was well treated by William Rufus's brother, Henry, who now took the throne – enough to rouse suspicion. Accident or murder? We are unlikely ever to know.

Her Majesty's Royal Palace and fortress: The Tower of London

- The Normans built a string of some 200 mighty stone fortresses across England, to control their conquered lands. They included Windsor Castle and Dover Castle. But chief among them was the Tower of London, built to protect their capital, London.

- The central defensive building, the White Tower, is the old keep, the main stronghold. Originally built in 1078, its walls are 27.4 m (90 ft) tall and 4.6 m (15 ft) thick at the base.

- The Tower of London is still considered one of the most secure places in Britain: that is why the Crown Jewels are kept here.

- Yeoman Warders (known as Beefeaters) guard the Tower, wearing a version of a uniform that dates back Henry VIII's time.

- Ravens are kept at the Tower. It is said that if they ever left, the monarchy would collapse.

- Henry I was the first king to use the Tower as a place to lock up high-ranking prisoners: the first prisoner was Ranulf Flambard, Bishop of Durham, who was also one of the very few prisoners ever to escape.

- The Bloody Tower, built in the 1220s, was used to house prisoners. It is so called because this is where the Princes in the Tower were lodged and supposedly murdered in 1483.

The six ravens on duty at the Tower today are great mimics: one can bark like a dog, while another says 'hello' in an eerily deep voice.

Woof!

The *White Ship*

On a still night on 25 November, 1120, the *White Ship* set sail for England from France. On board were many young members of the royal family, including the young Duke of Normandy, William Adelin, aged 22, the son and heir of Henry I. A short distance out of the harbour, the ship ran into rocks and capsized. The sole survivor was a French butcher. 'No ship ever brought so much misery to England,' wrote William of Malmesbury.

Henry I: 1100–1135

Henry succeeded his brother William Rufus. He married Matilda of Scotland, daughter of Malcolm III and St Margaret. Like all the Norman kings he was ruthless, and in 1106 he defeated and imprisoned his brother Robert. Henry died in France, aged 66, after eating too many lampreys (a kind of eel).

Stephen: 1135–1154

The grandson of William I, Stephen contested the throne in a civil war with Matilda, daughter of Henry I. His reign was a mess, dubbed 'The Nineteen-Year Winter'. When the war ended in 1153, Stephen was under the control of his unruly barons.

The Anarchy

Henry I and Matilda had two children: a daughter also called Matilda (or Maude), and a son, William Adelin. Matilda was married off to Henry V, the Holy Roman Emperor, in 1114 – a major triumph in royal networking. But Emperor Henry died in 1125. When William drowned in the *White Ship*, Henry appointed his daughter Matilda as his heir, and then made his barons swear an oath of allegiance to her. Matilda then married Geoffrey V, Count of Anjou (western France), and they had two sons; the oldest, Henry, was born in 1133.

When Henry I died, however, the barons decided they did not fancy being ruled by a woman: they renounced their oaths and backed Matilda's cousin Stephen of Blois, grandson of William I. The result was a period of civil war, called the Anarchy. Highlights included:

- Matilda defeated Stephen at the Battle of Lincoln in 1141, and marched to London to grab the crown. But she had to flee when the Londoners revolted.

- Stephen trapped Matilda in Oxford Castle in the winter of 1141, but she escaped in the snow, dressed in white.

- Stephen and Matilda finally negotiated a settlement in 1153: Stephen took power, but his son Eustace died before him. So he agreed to make Matilda's son Henry his heir.

List of early Plantagenet kings
1154–1399

Henry II, 1154–1189: son of Matilda
Richard I 'The Lionheart', 1189–1199: son of Henry II
John, 1199–1216: son of Henry II
Henry III, 1216–1272: son of John
Edward I 'Longshanks', 1272–1307: son of Henry III
Edward II, 1307–1327: son of Edward I
Edward III, 1327–1377: son of Edward II
Richard II, 1377–1399: Grandson of Edward III

The Lions of England, royal standard of King Richard the Lionheart.

CHAPTER five

THE PLANTAGENETS

There is a wild shrub called broom, with scented yellow flowers. It is called *genêt* in French. The story goes that Geoffrey V of Anjou, father of Henry II, picked a branch of broom and 'planted' it in his helmet as he went into battle, so he could be identified by his troops, hence creating the family name 'Plantagenet'. The first king, Henry II, came to rule a kingdom far bigger than any of his predecessors': it consisted of England, Wales and Ireland, as well as Anjou, Normandy, Brittany and Aquitaine – that is to say, about half of France.

Henry II: 1154–1189

Times were still turbulent when Henry II came to the throne – and he had a character to match: he was prone to tantrums of wild anger, and yet could also be charming and sophisticated. He was a man of action, but he was also a good administrator, and is credited for creating a fairer system of justice and taxation. His wife was the equally formidable Eleanor of Aquitaine. Essentially, after a good start to his reign, he caused such friction that things began to fall apart. His biggest quarrel was with his chancellor and Archbishop of Canterbury, Thomas à Becket – a power struggle between the Church and the Crown, which led to Thomas's infamous murder in 1170. Then Henry fought with Eleanor and his own sons.

The English Pope

In 1154, Nicholas Breakspear became Pope Adrian IV, the only English pope in history. He had reached this position of great power and influence by rising through the ranks of the Church in France and Italy. During his reign he gave Henry II the title 'Lord of Ireland' and permission to invade and rule it – or so Henry claimed. Adrian IV ruled for only five years before his death in 1159.

Murder in the Cathedral

'Will nobody rid me of this turbulent priest?' declared Henry II. Four knights took him at his word, rode to Canterbury and killed Thomas à Becket in the Cathedral. Henry was crippled with remorse, and had himself publicly flogged by monks in front of Becket's tomb. Thomas was declared a saint, and became the focus of fervent pilgrimage.

Richard the Lionheart: 1189–1199

When Henry II died, his son Richard inherited the throne – a heroic warrior who earned the nickname 'Lionheart'. Unfortunately, he directed his energies almost entirely abroad, fighting Crusades, and spent less than six months of his entire 10-year reign in England. When heading for home in 1192, he was captured by Leopold, Duke of Austria and had to be ransomed for a vast sum that virtually bankrupted England. Then he

Robin Hood

In the chaos of England in the days of Richard the Lionheart, the land was ruled by barons and petty tyrants such as the local sheriffs, in league with Richard's younger brother John. Arise the legend of Robin Hood, the cunning and saintly rebel. He was said to have been a nobleman whose lands were stolen by the cruel Sheriff of Nottingham. He and his band of Merry Men lived wild in Sherwood Forest, poaching deer and 'robbing the rich to give to the poor'. Robin Hood may not have existed, but the legend is probably based on real-life characters who survived in this way in the turmoil of the time.

headed back to France where he was shot in the shoulder by a bolt fired from a crossbow. The wound became infected and he died, aged 42, 12 days later. He was buried in Rouen cathedral, France.

Days of chivalry and the Crusades

In the 7th century Muslim armies overran the eastern Mediterranean and took control of the Holy Land, the site of the story of Christ, and the sacred lands of the Christians. In 1096, when Christian pilgrims to Jerusalem felt their access to the holy sites was being impeded, the Pope called for a holy war called the Crusades, pitching Christians against Muslims. There were at least seven Crusades in all. Richard the Lionheart took part in the Third, attempting (but failing) to retake Jerusalem from the Muslim leader Saladin.

A code of honour, called *chivalry*, developed around the knights who fought in the Crusades – a mixture of courage, fighting skills, Christian devotion, and loyalty. Popular poets and travelling musicians called *troubadours* sang about the virtues of good knights, and about their sense of pure devotion in love. Jousting tournaments, with knights mounted on horseback, became a favourite sport of the nobility – a sport in which all the virtues of chivalry could be displayed. The word 'chivalry', after all, comes from the French word for 'knight', *chevalier*, itself derived from *cheval*, meaning 'horse'.

John: 1199–1216

There is only one King of England called John – and with such a lousy reputation it is unlikely there will ever be another. John was Richard's younger brother. Richard died childless, so John came to the throne aged 32. He was notoriously greedy, cruel and incompetent. He managed to lose control of Normandy, and other French possessions. His haste and lack of judgement continued to the end of his days. Rushing to cross the Wash, the broad tidal estuary between Norfolk and Lincolnshire, his baggage train was caught by the incoming tide. He lost the crown jewels, and members of his staff were drowned. He died a few days later.

Q: Where did King John sign the Magna Carta?

A: At the bottom of the page.

In fact, he did not sign the Magna Carta at all. Like most kings of his era, he could not read or write (he had people to do that for him). Instead, he stamped the charter with the royal seal.

A landmark in British constitutional history, the Magna Carta (Great Charter) was stamped by King John at Runnymede, on the River Thames, in 1215. John had demanded piles of money from his barons to pay for his disastrous military campaigns. In the end, they rebelled and forced him to sign the Charter, which defined and limited the power of the king. John had no intention of respecting it, but over time it changed the way that kings and queens ruled Britain.

The first Parliament

In 1258, the nobles, bishops and other powerful figures in the land clubbed together to create a 'Privy Council' to advise the king, which Henry III reluctantly agreed to. Still the barons wanted greater control over the king, whom they thought guilty of misrule. In 1265 Henry's rebellious brother-in-law, Simon de Montfort, called on barons, knights, clergymen and town leaders to form a 'Parliament' – a term used for a kind of talking shop (from the French *parler*, meaning 'to speak'). Britain's modern parliament can trace its origins to this rough-and-ready ancestor.

Henry III: 1216–1272

Henry was just nine years old when he became a king, and reigned for 56 years. At first his kingdom was ruled well on his behalf by a regent, William Marshal, Earl of Pembroke. But Henry was less successful when he took control. He ran a series of disastrous military campaigns in France, and lost all remaining French possessions except Gascony. Henry III had a powerful belief that his powers were God-given, and rebuilt Westminster Abbey as a place where he and future kings could be buried and revered.

The Royal Zoo

Henry III was given three leopards by Emperor Frederick II; and the King of Norway gave him a polar bear. These formed the basis of a collection of exotic animals kept at the Tower of London, which the public could come and see. It was an attraction for 600 years, until the animals were transferred to the newly created London Zoo in 1832–1834.

Exotic pets have always been one of the perks of kingship, and often exchanged as gifts.

- Henry I had lions, leopards, lynxes and a porcupine.
- Richard II had a camel.
- Henry VII had a pet monkey.
- James VI (of Scotland) and I (of England) kept lions.
- George IV had a pet giraffe.
- George V had a parrot, which ate at the breakfast table.

Henry III's polar bear was allowed to go fishing in the Thames.

Edward I, 'Longshanks': 1272–1307

Henry's eldest son Edward was unusually tall, so he earned the nickname 'Longshanks' ('long legs'). At the age of 15 he married Eleanor of Castile. He was a warrior king, determined to bring order throughout the land, and to extend his power over Wales and Scotland – which earned him his other nickname: the 'Hammer of the Scots'. He imposed his authority by building a number of mighty castles, such as Caernarfon and Harlech in Wales. He died near Carlisle on his way to do battle with Robert the Bruce in Scotland.

The Coronation Chair and the Stone of Scone

In his first campaign in Scotland, Edward seized the Stone of Scone, the 'Stone of Destiny' on which Scottish kings had been crowned since Kenneth MacAlpin in 843. Edward I had a wooden chair made to fit over the stone – the throne on which all English monarchs have been crowned since 1308. The Stone of Scone, however, was removed from the throne in 1996 and restored to Scotland. It is now in Edinburgh Castle.

The Prince of Wales

The monarch's eldest son is called the Prince of Wales. This dates back to 1301, when Edward – having annexed Wales – gave the title to his 16-year-old son, the future Edward II. The emblem consists of three ostrich feathers and a coronet. This was first used by Edward the Black Prince (eldest son of Edward III), adopted perhaps from the family of his mother. The German motto *Ich Dien* ('I serve') may have come from the King of Bohemia, whom the Black Prince defeated at the Battle of Crécy in 1346.

Edward II: 1307–1327

In contrast to Edward I, his son Edward II was a disaster. At court he gave power and favours to handsome male friends. On the battlefield, Edward lost to Robert the Bruce and the Scots at the Battle of Bannockburn in 1314. In the end, Edward's wife, Isabella of France, and a group of exasperated nobles managed to depose him. Edward was held prisoner in Berkeley Castle, Gloucestershire, in terrible conditions until he was murdered.

foreign queens

The Plantagenet kings tended to marry foreign wives as part of the tradition of 'dynastic marriages' – using royal marriage to create beneficial diplomatic links. Here are the most notable of the medieval Queen Consorts:

Eleanor of Aquitaine (c. 1122–1204): married Henry II. Beautiful, clever, but also strong-willed, she was actually married to King Louis VII of France when she met Henry, and organised an annulment so she could marry him instead. She added vast French territories to the English crown. Later, she openly rebelled against Henry and was captured and imprisoned until his death in 1189.

Eleanor of Castile (c.1244–1290): married Edward I. Edward and Eleanor were devoted to each other, and Edward – unusually – remained loyal to her throughout their marriage, which took place when he was 15 and she was 13. They had 13 children. When she died, Edward set up a series of 12 stone crosses to mark where her body had rested, on its way to burial in Westminster Abbey; these included Charing Cross in London.

Isabella of France (1292–1358): married Edward II. She arrived in England at the age of 12 to discover that her husband preferred the company of men. Still, they managed to produce four children, including the future Edward III. Despised as the 'She-Wolf of France', she had an affair with Roger Mortimer, and together they disposed of Edward.

Philippa of Hainault (c.1314–1369): married Edward III. Daughter of the Count of Hainault (now part of Belgium), and his wife Jeanne de Valois, Philippa was a member of the French royal family. At their marriage in York Minster in 1328, she was 16 and he was 15. They had fourteen children, nine of whom survived infancy, including Edward the Black Prince and John of Gaunt (or Ghent, where he was born).

Catherine of Valois (1401–1437) married Henry V. Daughter of Charles VI of France, her marriage reinforced Henry's claim to the French throne, but he died before he could inherit it. She was the mother of Henry VI, and – through her second, secret marriage to Owen Tudor – grandmother of Henry VII. For 300 years after her death her mummified corpse was on display in Westminster Abbey.

Margaret of Anjou (1430–1482): married Henry VI. A formidable force, she rallied Lancastrian forces to defend her weak and mentally unstable husband during the Wars of the Roses, but in vain.

The Order of the Garter

Edward III's court was one of the most splendid in Europe, and also one of the most extravagant. Echoing the mood of elegant knightly chivalry, in about 1348 Edward II created the Order of the Garter, named after the blue and gold garter worn below the left knee. It remains today the highest award in the honours system. Membership is limited to the sovereign and the Prince of Wales, plus 24 Knights or Ladies Companion, chosen personally by the sovereign.

Edward III: 1327–1377

Edward was not yet 15 when his father was murdered – too young to take control just yet. So his mother Isabella and her lover Roger Mortimer ran the country, but he hated both of them. When nearly 18, he imprisoned his mother and had Mortimer executed. Edward was a successful warrior, particularly against the French. After his beloved wife Philippa died in 1369, he took up with the wife of one of his knights, the grasping and unpopular Alice Perrers. His warrior son the Black Prince died in 1376. By the time Edward himself died, the nation had become disenchanted.

The Hundred Years' War (1337~1453)

King Charles IV of France died without male heirs in 1328. His cousin, Philip de Valois, was placed on the throne, but there were other contenders, including Edward III – son of Isabella of France. In 1346 he won a great victory at the Battle of Crécy, noted as the first battle in which the English used cannons. Calais became an English possession. The war rumbled on and on, and only finally came to a close in 1453, 116 years after it had started.

The Black Prince

Edward III's eldest son was also called Edward (1330–76), and was nicknamed The Black Prince because he wore black armour. He was a famous and feared warrior, and a hero of numerous exploits, including the famous victories at Crécy in 1346 and at Poitiers in 1356. But the Black Prince was also celebrated for his fairness and chivalry. He returned home, exhausted and sick, in 1371, and died in 1376.

The Black Death

A great disaster struck England in 1348: plague arrived on the south coast and rapidly spread throughout the country. Over the next two years or so, at least one third of the population of England died. Whole villages were wiped out. The illness was swift and merciless; its cause is still a mystery to this day – earlier theories that it was bubonic plague spread by fleas on rats do not explain the speed with which it travelled and killed its victims. Further bouts of plague continued until the end of the century. For survivors, life became hard because of the drastic reduction in manpower. But it also changed society: people at the bottom of the labour market could now demand better terms for their work, and the feudal system became less rigid.

Richard II: 1377–1399

Grandson of Edward III, and the son of the Black Prince, Richard II was just 10 years old when he came to the throne, so his uncle, John of Gaunt, ruled in his place. Richard was a spoilt brat who grew into a cruel, arrogant king. His high-handed behaviour eventually caused a rebellion amongst the nobles, led by his cousin Henry Bolingbroke. Richard II died in prison – perhaps murdered, perhaps just starved to death. Bolingbroke took the throne as Henry IV. Not everyone approved: England was about to descend into a period of chaos...

The Peasants' Revolt

In 1381 England was seething with discontent. The big issue was a new poll tax, which put an unfair burden on the poor. Led by Wat Tyler, Jack Straw and John Ball, thousands of peasants marched to London. They stormed the Tower of London, seized the Archbishop of Canterbury and other officials, and chopped off their heads. Richard II, aged just 14, rode to Smithfield to confront the rebels, and at the meeting Wat Tyler was attacked and killed. To disperse the crowds, Richard made promises which he later withdrew. The other leaders were executed.

List of Scottish kings and queens
1057–1371

HOUSE OF CANMORE (1057–1290)
Malcolm III 'Canmore', 1057–1093: son of
   Duncan I
Donald III, 'Donald Bane', 1093–1094: son of
   Duncan I
Duncan II, 1094: son of Malcolm III
Donald III (restored), 1094–1097
Edgar, 1097–1107: son of Malcolm III
Alexander I 'The Fierce', 1107–1124: son of
   Malcolm III
David I, 1124–1153: son of Malcolm III
Malcolm IV 'The Maiden', 1153–1165:
   grandson of David I
William I 'The Lion', 1165 –1214: grandson
   of David I
Alexander II, 1214–1249: son of William I
Alexander III, 1249–1286: son of Alexander II
Margaret, 'Maid of Norway', 1286–1290:
   granddaughter of Alexander III

HOUSE OF BALLIOL
John Balliol, 1292–1296: great-great-great-
   grandson of David I

*Interregnum: Edward I of England governs
Scotland directly.*

HOUSE OF BRUCE (1306–1371)
Robert I 'The Bruce', 1306–1329: great-
   great-great-great-grandson of David I
David II, 1329–1371: son of Robert I

CHAPTER SIX

CANMORE, WALLACE & BRUCE

The struggle for succession in the early 11th century saw the deaths in battle of Duncan I, Macbeth and Lulach, as the House of Dunkeld finally fell to Malcolm Canmore (Malcolm III), the first king of the House of Canmore (the word means 'big head' or 'big chief' in Gaelic). Following the Norman Conquest in 1066, the Scottish kings entered into an uneasy and often bloody power struggle with the kings of England. Eventually resentment turned into open rebellion led by William Wallace and Robert the Bruce against the intrusions of Edward I and Edward III of England.

Malcolm III (1057–1093) had close contacts with English nobles who had fled north to Scotland following the Norman Conquest. In 1069 he married Margaret, from the House of Wessex. Switching between submission and aggression, he launched periodic raids on Norman England until he was killed at Alnwick in Northumbria in 1093. Margaret (later called St Margaret of Scotland) is said to have died of a broken heart.

Malcolm III was succeeded by his brother **Donald Bane** (1093–1094), claiming the legitimacy of tanistry. He was soon ousted by **Duncan II** (1094), son of Malcolm II and Margaret, who had the backing of William Rufus of England. Scotland was now torn between claimants who leant towards England and those who resisted this foreign influence.

Three further sons of Malcolm II and Margaret reigned in quick succession:

- **Edgar 'The Valiant' (1097–1107) reunited Scotland with the help of English forces, defeating and blinding Donald Bane – who may have disagreed with Edgar's nickname.**

- **Alexander I (1107–1124)** was called 'The Fierce' because of his brutal suppression of a revolt in Moray.
- **David I (1124–1153)**

The last of these, **David I**, is ranked as one of the greatest Scottish kings. He had been brought up in the court of Henry I of England, and married into the family of the Earl of Northumbria. He encouraged trade with the Dutch and minted the first Scottish coins.

Trews and kilts

Edgar the Valiant made peace with the northern Vikings led by Magnus Barelegs, granting him power over the islands of the Hebrides. Magnus's nickname related to his clothing: he wore a kind of kilt – one of the earliest references to this style of garment. The people of Alba (Gaelic Scotland), for their part, wore tunics and trousers, or 'trews'. The modern short kilt evolved in the 19th century from the belted plaid worn by men of the Highlands: a huge length of cloth wrapped around the body and over the shoulder, with a belt around the waist.

Then:

- Malcolm IV 'The Maiden' (1153–1165) lost Northumbria again. He took a vow of chastity, hence the unflattering nickname.

- William I 'The Lion' (1165–1214) was defeated and captured on another raid into England. The price of release was submission to Henry I, but he bought Scotland's independence by donating a colossal sum of money to Richard I's Crusade.

- Alexander II (1214–1249) married Joan, daughter of King John of England, and fixed the Scottish border to more or less its present line from the River Tweed to the Solway Firth.

- Alexander III (1249–1286) succeeded to the throne aged 8, and married Henry III's daughter Margaret in 1251, when he was 10 and she was 11. His reign was a golden age in Scotland, and a time of prosperity matched by cordial relations with the English king, Edward I. Alexander defeated the Vikings at sea in the Battle of Largs in 1263, and won back the Hebrides. He died when he and his horse fell over a cliff.

- Margaret, the 'Maid of Norway' (1286–1290), ruled as a child.

Margaret, the 'Maid of Norway'

In 1274, Alexander III lost his wife, and then, between 1281 and 1284, all three of their children died. One of these was his daughter Margaret, who was married to Erik II, King of Norway. She died after giving birth to a daughter, also called Margaret. When aged 3 and still in Norway, little Margaret succeeded to the throne of Scotland upon the death of her grandfather, Alexander III. Edward I of England proposed an arranged marriage between Margaret and his own son. But on her way to Scotland from Norway, aged 6, Margaret was overcome by seasickness and died.

With the death of the Maid of Norway, the House of Canmore came to an end, leaving a power vacuum in Scotland, and 13 claimants to the throne. A Scottish nobleman called **John Balliol** (1292–1296) won the contest, with the backing of Edward I of England. But when Edward I demanded Scottish troops to fight the French, John Balliol refused; instead he signed a treaty with France – the start of the special relationship between Scotland and France known as the 'Auld Alliance'. In 1296,

Edward I crushed the Scots at the very bloody Battle of Dunbar.

Edward I, the 'Hammer of the Scots', now ruled over Scotland directly. To add insult to injury, he seized the Stone of Scone and took it back to England. When the Scots rebelled in 1298, Edward marched north and won a resounding victory at the Battle of Falkirk. He returned in 1303 to face the new leader of the Scots, William Wallace.

William Wallace

William Wallace, the son of a minor Scottish knight, was an outlaw. The charge was the murder of an English sheriff who had killed Wallace's companion (or wife). Wallace quickly gathered huge popular support. In 1297 his rag-tag army took on the English at the Battle of Stirling Bridge and won a resounding victory. Wallace refused the crown, but accepted the title Guardian of Scotland. Meanwhile, Edward I assembled a massive army and the two armies clashed at the Battle of Falkirk in 1298. Wallace was defeated and went into hiding. He was betrayed and captured in 1305. He was put to death in London as a traitor, in the most gruesome manner.

attle of Stirling Bridge, 1297

After Wallace's defeat, Robert the Bruce took over as Guardian of Scotland, sharing the role with John Comyn. Robert (the old family name was de Brus) had royal connections: he was the great-great-great-great-grandson of David I. In 1306 he arranged to meet John Comyn in Greyfriars Church, Dumfries, and stabbed him to death. He then had himself crowned at Scone as **Robert I** (1306–1329).

Robert skirmished with the English until, in the summer of 1307, Edward I died. When Edward II marched on Scotland in 1314, Robert trounced the English at the Battle of Bannockburn. Robert gradually won back Scotland, and its independence was pronounced in the Declaration of Arbroath of 1320.

When Robert died in 1329, his son **David II** (1329–1371) inherited the throne, aged 5. A series of battles with the English led to David's capture in 1346, and he was held by the English until a ransom was paid in 1357. Meanwhile his nephew Robert Stewart (a grandson of Robert the Bruce) ruled in his stead, and when David died without heir in 1371, the crown passed to Robert. So began the House of Stewart.

Robert the Bruce
and the spider

Edward I was not at all pleased to hear that there was a new, self-appointed king of Scotland. Back he came with his armies, and put Robert to flight. Now an outlaw in hiding, Robert was sitting in a cave one winter's day, contemplating his desperate situation, when he saw a spider – or so the legend goes. He watched it busily trying to make its web: six times it failed before at last it succeeded. From this Robert took the lesson that, with patient persistence, he could succeed in defeating the English.

Try, try and try again...

The spider also taught Robert how to get to sleep when you know there's a spider in your room.

List of later Plantagenet kings
1399–1485

HOUSE OF LANCASTER (1399–1461)

Henry IV, 1399–1413: grandson of Edward III
Henry V, 1413–1422: son of Henry IV
Henry VI, 1422–1461, 1470–1471: son of
  Henry V

HOUSE OF YORK (1461–1485)

Edward IV, 1461–1470, 1471–1483: great-
  great-grandson of Edward III
Edward V, 1483: son of Edward IV
Richard III, 1483–1485: brother of Edward IV

The White Rose   The Red Rose

House of York   House of Lancaster

CHAPTER SEVEN

YORKISTS & LANCASTRIANS

So, back in England, Henry IV had seized the throne by having Richard II bumped off. As the son of John of Gaunt, Henry was also Duke of Lancaster. The trouble was, John of Gaunt had an older brother, Edmund of Langley, who was the Duke of York, and *he* had a son called Richard. This led to a long-term rivalry between the House of Lancaster and the House of York, which was resolved only in 1485. Meanwhile, the Hundred Years' War with France was *still* rumbling on.

Henry IV: 1399–1413

As Henry was not the universal choice for king, he was in constant fear of rebellion. He faced many revolts, but Parliament supported him and agreed that his son Henry should be the next king.

Henry V: 1413–1422

The young and ambitious warrior king Henry V scored a number of famous victories against the French, including the Battle of Agincourt. He spent most of his reign abroad, and in 1420

The Battle of Agincourt

In 1415, on his retreat to England from a failed siege in northern France, Henry V ran into the French army blocking his route to Calais. The French had 20,000 men; Henry V had 5,000 archers – using the deadly longbow – and 900 other soldiers. When the French cavalry charged into boggy ground, they were destroyed by a hail of arrows. It was one of the most famous English victories.

became the heir to the French throne, and promptly married Catherine of Valois, daughter of Charles VI of France – but before he could inherit, he died at the age of 35, from dysentery.

Henry VI (Part 1): 1422–1461

So Henry V's son took over – at the age of just 9 months. He grew up to be a serious, delicate soul, deeply moral and religious, and perhaps mentally ill. He lost English possessions in France as the French gathered strength under the inspired leadership of Joan of Arc. Back home, his cousin, Richard, Duke of York, launched a civil war: defeated, Henry VI fled to Scotland, and Edward, the son of Richard of York, became Edward IV.

Edward IV (Part 1): 1461–1470

Edward IV was very tall for his time (6 ft 3 in; 1.9 m); and he was handsome, a successful warrior and a good diplomat. But he was also determined to have his way. This included secretly marrying a young widow called Elizabeth Woodville, then favouring her relatives. When the powerbroker, Richard Neville, Earl of Warwick ('the Kingmaker'), switched sides to support the Lancastrians, other nobles rebelled and Edward fled abroad.

Henry VI (Part 2): 1470–1471

So Henry VI came back for a second time. Mistake: he proved even more hopeless than before. Edward IV returned from France with Burgundian troops and defeated Henry at the Battle of Tewkesbury, killing his son, 18-year-old Edward, Prince of Wales. Henry was imprisoned in the Tower of London, where he was murdered.

Edward IV (Part 2): 1471–1483

Second time round, Edward behaved a lot better. He made peace with the French and the Scots, reduced taxes, and allowed trade to flourish. Happy days… until Edward dropped dead at the age of 40, without having properly secured the succession for his son, 12-year-old Prince Edward.

Edward V: 1483

So little Prince Edward became king… although he was never crowned. He was placed in the care of his uncle Richard, Duke of Gloucester, who had other ideas. Edward was lodged in the Tower of London with his little brother. They only lasted three months.

The Princes in the Tower

In 1483, the boy king Edward V, aged 12, and his younger brother Richard, Duke of York, aged 10, were murdered in the Tower of London – probably. Few people knew about this at the time, although they had their suspicions. Their uncle, Richard, Duke of Gloucester, had taken the two princes into his care after the death of their father, Edward IV: Richard had feared of that the princes would come under the control of their power-hungry mother, Elizabeth Woodville. So he put them in the Tower, which served as both a highly secure residence and a prison. Meanwhile, Richard persuaded Parliament to declare that the marriage of Edward IV to Elizabeth Woodville had been illegal, so their sons, the princes, were not true heirs to the throne. Thus Richard became king as Richard III.

Evidence of murder only came to light when bones were discovered in 1674 (and more in the 1980s). Who did it? Fingers were pointed at Richard III, who clearly had the most to gain. But nothing has ever been proved. We shall probably never know.

Richard III

You'll be hearing from my lawyers, Mr Shakespeare... and my lawyers have *swords*.

The Wars of the Roses

Two cousins, two rival families... Edward of York versus Henry VI, from the House of Lancaster. Both claimed the crown as descendants of Edward III. The result was a civil war that ran on and off for over 30 years, between about 1455 and 1485. Highlights included:

Yorkists triumph! In July 1460, Henry VI is captured at the Battle of Northampton.

Lancastrians triumph! In December 1460, Richard, Duke of York, is defeated and killed at the Battle of Wakefield.

Yorkists triumph! In 1461, Henry VI is defeated at the Battle of Towton, and Edward (eldest son of the old Duke of York) becomes Edward IV.

Yorkists triumph! In 1471, at the Battle of Barnet, Edward IV defeats the turncoat Earl of Warwick ('the Kingmaker'), who is killed.

Lancastrians triumph! In 1470, nobles rebel against Edward IV, who flees to France; Henry VI is restored to the throne.

Yorkists triumph! In 1471, at the very bloody Battle of Tewkesbury, Henry VI is defeated and his son Prince Edward is killed.

Lancastrians triumph! In 1485, at the Battle of Bosworth Field, Henry Tudor defeats and kills Richard III.

Richard III: 1483–1485

In many ways Richard III was a good king: a brave and successful warrior, who promised to be fair to his people. But he had plenty of enemies, including the House of Lancaster. One of these was Henry Tudor, a descendant of John of Gaunt. Henry brought an army from France, landed in Wales, and confronted Richard at the Battle of Bosworth Field, in Leicestershire. Richard was killed, his army defeated. It was the end of the Wars of the Roses, and the beginning of a new era.

Bad press

Name the most unpopular, cruel, evil, demented king in English history. Richard III? You mean the one nicknamed 'Richard Crookback', because of his supposed deformed back and withered arm? The one who murdered his little nephews? Much of Richard III's reputation today comes from Shakespeare's portrayal of him in his play *Richard the Third*. It served the Tudors well to paint Richard as a twisted tyrant who utterly deserved his fate. But even in his day Richard was reviled. His dead body was stripped and tipped into a simple church grave. Later even that was dug up, and his bones thrown into a river – the ultimate disrespect.

List of Tudor Kings and Queens
1485–1603

Henry VII, 1485–1509: great-great-grandson of Edward III
Henry VIII, 1509–1547: son of Henry VII
Edward VI, 1547–1553: son of Henry VIII
Jane Grey, 1553: great-granddaughter of Henry VII
Mary I (Bloody Mary), 1553–1558: daughter of Henry VIII
Elizabeth I, 1558–1603: daughter of Henry VIII

Q: Which one of Henry VIII's wives cooked with herbs?

A: Catherine of Tarragon

CHAPTER EIGHT

THE TUDORS

Peace at last... well, almost. The torment of the Wars of the Roses had come to a close. Henry Tudor, from the House of Lancaster, became Henry VII, and – as a gesture of goodwill – he married Elizabeth of York, daughter of Edward IV. During Tudor times, England prospered and grew in power, and began to enjoy some of the cultural sophistication of the European Renaissance, a watershed between the medieval and modern worlds. But the new problem in Europe was religion: the powerful Catholic Church was about to splinter.

Henry VII 1485–1509

Henry was the great-great-grandson of John of Gaunt (the fourth son of Edward III) and his third wife – so his claim to the throne was extremely weak. But England was too exhausted by three decades of war to complain. Through good management, he brought stability and prosperity to the nation. Although his marriage with Elizabeth of York was arranged, they became deeply fond of one another, and Henry was devastated when she died in 1503.

The pretenders

Several people tried to contest Henry's claim to the throne. At the age of about 10, Lambert Simnel was identified by Yorkist rebels as the nephew of Edward IV. He was crowned king in Ireland, but was captured after a battle in Nottinghamshire in 1487. Henry pardoned him and gave him a job as a spit-turner in the royal kitchens. Perkin Warbeck was a conman who claimed he was Edward V, one of the Princes in the Tower. With the support of Margaret of York, Duchess of Burgundy, he invaded England twice. After his defeat in 1497, he was imprisoned in the Tower, then hanged after trying to escape.

Real tennis

Henry VII played real tennis, and made it into a fashionable game. It was played in an indoor court, surrounded by walls, with a net in the middle. The name 'real' is thought to come from the Spanish for 'royal'. Henry VIII was also an enthusiastic player: he was apparently playing tennis when news of Anne Boleyn's execution was brought to him. His court can still be seen at Hampton Court Palace. The modern game of lawn tennis was not invented until some 400 years later.

Henry VIII: 1509–1547

Things started out pretty well for Henry VIII, who was just 17 years old when his father died. He was every bit the Renaissance prince – bright, brave, dashing. He loved music, wrote books, played tennis and was good at jousting. He was rich and fashionable, and happily married to Catherine of Aragon. He ran the country well and started to create a very effective navy. But then things turned sour. He desperately needed a son, to make sure he could pass on the Tudor legacy. He set his path on divorcing Catherine, which caused a mighty rift with the Catholic Church. He then ploughed through five more wives, executed a series of close advisors, and grew disgustingly fat, diseased and bad-tempered. By the time England's most famous king died, aged 55, most people were glad to see the back of him.

The field of the Cloth of Gold

Henry VIII had big ambitions for England: he wanted to make it as powerful as France, Spain and the Holy Roman Empire – the three big powers in Europe. In 1520, he arranged to meet with Francis I, King of France, near Calais, which was still an English possession. He put on a fantastic show of wealth and extravagance, which became known as the Field of the Cloth of Gold. But in 1522 Henry returned to old English habits, waging war on France, without much success.

His Majesty

Henry VIII was the first English king to be called 'Your Majesty' – somewhat typical of his inflated view of his own glory.

Of course I'm majestic! How could I *not* be majestic!?

Henry VIII's palaces

Henry inherited a number of palaces, and had several built for him:

The Palace of Westminster: Built for Edward the Confessor in about 1045–1050, Westminster became the main royal residence in London until 1512, when a fire caused Henry to move to nearby Whitehall. It has been the seat of Parliament ever since the 13th century. Most of the old Palace burnt down in 1834: of the original, only Westminster Hall and the Jewel Tower remain.

Whitehall Palace: Built as the London residence of the Archbishop of York, it came into the hands of Cardinal Wolsey, who developed it as a fine residence; after his downfall in 1529, Henry VIII seized it and added tennis courts, a bowling alley, and a tiltyard for jousting. With 1,500 rooms over a sprawling site, it became one of the largest palaces of the day. Most of it burnt down in 1698, but the Banqueting Hall, completed for Charles I in 1622, survives.

Hampton Court Palace: Thomas (later Cardinal) Wolsey bought this house in 1514, developed it into a splendid palace, and gave it to Henry VIII in 1525. It was updated by Sir Christopher Wren for James II and William and Mary, and completed for George II. The famous maze dates from 1702.

Bridewell Palace (close to Blackfriars Bridge, London): This was Henry VIII's main residence from 1515 to 1523. Divorce proceedings against Catherine of Aragon were conducted here in 1528. Henry abandoned it in 1530, and Edward VI gave it to the City of London. It became a refuge for the homeless in 1556, then a prison, workhouse and hospital. It was destroyed in the Great Fire of London in 1666.

St James's Palace: Originally built for Henry VIII in 1536, when it stood in fields outside London, it was the favoured residence of Mary I. It became the official royal residence after Whitehall Palace was destroyed by fire in 1698, cherished by James II, Anne, George II and Victoria in particular. It is still used to host numerous ceremonial functions.

The privy
When Henry VIII went to the loo, he sat on his 'privy', a word connected with the idea of privacy. A portable version was called a 'close stool' – a box with a padded velvet seat, and a hole over a chamber pot. The honour of attending His Majesty in these intimate moments was accorded to noblemen of high rank and trustworthiness, called the gentlemen of the Privy Chamber, and led by the Groom of the Stool.

The Six wives of Henry VIII

'Divorced, beheaded, died,
divorced, beheaded, survived.'

Catherine of Aragon (1485–1536).
Formerly married to Henry's older
brother Arthur, Catherine was a
Spanish princess and never lost her
accent. They married in 1509; he
was 17, and she was now 23. Despite the age
difference, they were devoted to each other.
They had a son in 1511, but he died after a few
weeks. In 1516 they had a daughter, Mary
(later Queen Mary I); she was the only
surviving child of six pregnancies. But Henry
decided he just had to have a son, so he needed a
new wife. After 18 years they **DIVORCED**.

Anne Boleyn (c.1507–1536). An
attractive daughter of one of
Catherine's maids of honour, Anne
was some 15 years younger than
Henry. Eight months after they were secretly
married, they had a daughter, Elizabeth (later
Queen Elizabeth I). Further pregnancies ended
in miscarriages. After three years, Henry –
still desperate for a son – accused her of
infidelity. She was tried and **BEHEADED**.

Jane Seymour (1508–1537). They
married just eleven days after Anne
was beheaded. Jane was 27, Henry
was now 45. The following year,

1537, she gave birth to a son, Edward, the future King Edward VI. Hurrah! But a few days after his birth, she **DIED**.

Anne of Cleves (1515–1557). In 1540, Henry decided to make a diplomatic foreign marriage with a German princess. Encouraged by Thomas Cromwell, he sent his court painter, Hans Holbein the Younger, to make a portrait of her, and liked what he saw. But the painting flattered Anne. He couldn't bear the sight of her in the flesh. After six months the marriage was annulled, so they were **DIVORCED**.

Catherine Howard (1520–1542). The niece of the Duke of Norfolk, Catherine was 19 when she married Henry just a couple of weeks after his divorce from Anne of Cleves. This marriage lasted just 18 months before Henry became jealous of her previous loves and accused her of infidelity – not without reason, it seems. She was **BEHEADED**.

Catherine Parr (1512–1548). By this time Henry was not a great marriage prospect. He was lucky enough to find a pleasant widow, in her early 30s, who would take him on. They married in 1543, Henry died in 1547... and so she **SURVIVED**.

The break with Rome

All across Europe Protestants were rebelling against the Catholic Church, especially after the German priest Martin Luther published his complaints in 1517. At first, Henry VIII would have none of it, and was even designated 'Defender of the Faith' by the Pope in Rome for his robust rejection of Martin Luther's message. But breaking away from the Catholic Church brought two important advantages to Henry: he no longer needed the permission of the Pope to divorce his wife Catherine of Aragon, and he could grab the fabulous riches of the Catholic Churches in England – Church treasures, monastery buildings, and vast tracts of lands.

So Henry joined the Protestant Revolt or 'Reformation' and created the Church of England. Between 1536 and 1540 Henry, assisted by his chancellor Thomas Cromwell, systematically destroyed most of the great Church institutions of England and Wales, in a programme called the 'Dissolution of the Monasteries'. Henry kept the spoils, or handed them out to his loyal supporters.

The four Thomases

Thomas Wolsey (c.1472–1530): Said to have been the son of a butcher, Wolsey became Henry's Lord Chancellor, Archbishop of York and a Cardinal in the Church of Rome. He built Hampton Court as his own palace. Henry gave him the job of persuading the Pope to permit his divorce from Catherine of Aragon, but he failed. **ARRESTED; DIED ON HIS WAY TO THE TRIAL.**

Thomas More (1478–1535): St Thomas to some – a man of great learning and high morals, he became Lord Chancellor after Thomas Cromwell. But he could not accept Henry's divorce from Catherine of Aragon and the break with Rome. **BEHEADED.**

Thomas Cromwell (c.1485–1540): The son of a clothworker, he rose to become Henry's Chancellor through brilliance and cunning. He devised the plan for stripping the Catholic Church of its possessions, making Henry and himself hugely rich – but he made the mistake of advising Henry to marry Anne of Cleves. **BEHEADED.**

Thomas Cranmer (1489–1556): Henry's Archbishop of Canterbury, he smoothed the path for his divorce from Catherine of Aragon and the break with Rome. **BURNT AT THE STAKE BY MARY I.**

Edward VI: 1547–1553

Unfortunately, Henry's only son and heir was a sickly kid – and he was just nine years old. He was deeply religious, and was determined to turn England into a thoroughly Protestant land. Powerful forces lined up to assist him: first his uncle Edward Seymour served as Lord Protector, until he was executed in 1549, then it was John Dudley, Earl of Warwick (and later Duke of Northumberland). Before he could secure his plan, Edward died, aged 15, of an unidentified lung disease.

Lady Jane Grey

John Dudley tried to prevent Mary from taking the throne. He persuaded the dying Edward to approve the succession of 16-year-old Lady Jane Grey, the Protestant great-granddaughter of Henry VII – and also the wife of Dudley's son. She was crowned in 1553. Mary swiftly raised an army and marched on London. Jane Grey, the reluctant 'nine days' queen', handed over the crown. Nonetheless, she was imprisoned in the Tower of London. Dudley was beheaded, and in 1554 Jane and her husband were tried for treason and also beheaded. The reign of 'Bloody Mary' had begun.

Mary I: 1553–1558

Next in line was Henry VIII's oldest daughter, Mary. She was Roman Catholic. You might say that Mary had an axe to grind. She saw herself as the true heir to the throne: after the illegal divorce of her mother from Henry VIII, no other heirs should have counted. She was also fervently Roman Catholic, and determined to save her Church from Protestantism. In 1554, she married Philip II of Spain, an equally fervent Catholic; he was 27, she was 37. Mary tried to help Philip in his wars against the French, but only succeeded in losing Calais in 1558 – England's last foothold in France. When she died childless, at the age of 42, England rejoiced.

Mary I and
Philip II of Spain

Elizabeth I: 1558–1603

So another of Henry VIII's children came to the throne: Elizabeth, the 25-year-old daughter of Anne Boleyn, and a Protestant. Red-haired and pretty, she was charismatic, fashionable and wise, but she could also be ruthless. Her cousin, Mary, Queen of Scots, was next in line to the throne: fearing that Mary was plotting against her, Elizabeth kept her under house arrest for nearly 20 years, and then, in 1587, had her executed. Elizabeth I's reign of 45 years is seen as a 'golden age' in which Britain prospered, and grew in self-confidence as a world power.

A right royal stink

Queen Elizabeth had a wardrobe of some 3,000 dresses. Many of them were extremely elaborate, padded and quilted in silk and covered with embroidery and jewelry – too elaborate to wash properly. But that didn't matter much: the Elizabethans used perfumes to hide the smell of body odour, which mingled with the stench of chamber pots and sewers. They did not bathe often. Queen Elizabeth, however, was considered unusually clean. She declared proudly that she bathed once a month 'whether I need it or not.'

'I know I have the body but of a weak and feeble woman, but I have the heart and stomach of a king, and of a king of England too.'

Queen Elizabeth I, addressing her assembled forces at Tilbury as the Spanish Armada approached.

The Spanish Armada

Philip II of Spain, former husband of Mary I, decided that he had the right to run England, and won the support of the Pope to crush this upstart Protestant nation, ruled by a queen. He assembled a fleet of 130 huge ships, called the Armada, and in 1588 he sent it off to invade England, carrying an army of 17,000 soldiers.

The English had a fleet of 200 smaller, more mobile ships, under the command of Lord Howard of Effingham. The swashbuckling adventurer Sir Francis Drake was second in command. According to legend, he was playing bowls in Plymouth when news of the Armada's approach came; he calmly insisted on finishing his game first.

The Armada headed to Calais, where it sat at anchor to pick up more troops from the Spanish Netherlands. The English sent eight burning boats toward the Spanish fleet. When the Armada tried to flee from the flames, it was attacked off Gravelines and quickly routed. Then a terrible storm scattered the Armada and drove the Spanish ships north, to be wrecked on the coasts of Scotland and Ireland. Altogether the Spanish lost 70 ships and over half of their men. English ships lost: 0. It was one of England's most famous and important victories.

The Queen's favourites

Elizabeth I courted a number of favourites. Some may have hoped for marriage, but she never did marry – hence she was known as the 'Virgin Queen'.

Robert Dudley, 1st Earl of Leicester (1532–1588)

Any thought of marriage had to be abandoned after Dudley's wife Amy Robsart died in suspicious circumstances in 1560 (falling down stairs). When Dudley married again in 1588, Elizabeth was furious, but she eventually forgave him.

Sir Christopher Hatton (1540–1591)

Handsome and a good dancer, Christopher Hatton drew Elizabeth's eye. His devotion to her led to his appointments as Vice-Chamberlain of the Household and Privy Councillor, and later Lord Chancellor.

Sir Walter Raleigh (c.1554–1618)

Soldier, sailor and explorer, Raleigh supposedly threw his cloak down in a puddle in front of Elizabeth, so that she wouldn't get her feet wet. But she imprisoned him in the Tower of London briefly when he secretly married one of her maids-of-honour, Elizabeth Throckmorton.

William Shakespeare

Queen Elizabeth I loved the theatre, and with her encouragement the theatre in England flourished. She even sponsored a theatre troupe called Queen Elizabeth's Men, formed in 1583. The outstanding star of Elizabethan theatre was William Shakespeare (1564–1616), whose work in London was performed at the new public theatres such as The Rose (built 1587) and The Globe (1599). Elizabeth clearly saw some of his plays: she apparently enjoyed the jolly character of Falstaff in *Henry IV Part 1*, and Shakespeare may have written him into *The Merry Wives of Windsor* for her pleasure.

Royal names around the world

Sir Walter Raleigh is believed to have named the US state of Virginia after Elizabeth I, the 'Virgin Queen'. As a result of the British exploration, settlement and colonisation that took place from the 16th century onwards, countless places around the world have names with royal connections. Here are just ten of them:

Maryland, USA: named after Mary I

Georgia, USA: named after George II

Jamestown (the first permanent English settlement in North America): named in 1607 after James VI & I

New York: after the Province of New York, named in 1664 after James, Duke of York (the future James II)

Williamsburg, Virginia: named after William III (and Mary)

Adelaide, Australia: named after the Queen consort of William IV

Georgetown, Guyana: named after George III

Prince Edward Island, Canada: named after Prince Edward Augustus, fourth son of George III and father of Queen Victoria

Victoria Falls: named after Queen Victoria

Victoria, Australia (state): named after Queen Victoria

List of Stewart kings and queens of Scotland
1371–1625

Robert II, 1371–1390: grandson of Robert I
Robert III, 1390–1406: son of Robert II
James I, 1406–1437: son of Robert III
James II, 1437–1460: son of James I
James III, 1460–1488: son of James II
James IV, 1488–1513: son of James III
James V, 1513–1542: son of James IV
Mary Queen of Scots, 1542–1567: daughter of James V
James VI, 1567–1625: son of Mary

Earl of Arran, Regent

Earl of Lennox

Earl of Argyll

That crown should have been mine!

Mary, Queen of Scots was just a 9-month-old baby when she was crowned queen!

CHAPTER NINE

WHAT'S UP IN SCOTLAND?

et's go back to 1371, when Robert Stewart became Robert II. He came from a family that held the hereditary title of High Steward of Scotland, which dated back 200 years to the reign of David I. These were tough times. When the Kings of Scotland weren't battling against England, they had to deal with the ambitions of rival families and nobles, often brutally dispatching them with imprisonment, exile and murder. Meanwhile, repeated bouts of plague (1349, 1361–2, 1379 and 1392), wiped out about one third of the Scottish population.

Robert II (1371–1390) had a fairly uneventful reign, during which he secured succession by fathering 21 children. Unusually for a Scottish king, he died of old age. Then things got worse:

- **Robert III** (1390–1406): Invalided by a kick from a horse in 1388, he was bedevilled by his brother Robert, Duke of Albany, who imprisoned Robert's son and starved him to death. Robert sent his second son James to France for his protection, but James was held captive in the Tower of London for 18 years. Robert is said to have died of grief.

- **James I** (1406–1437): Still held captive for the first 16 years of his reign, he was ransomed in 1424. James 'the Lawgiver' then ruled firmly, until he was murdered in the castle sewer in Perth by a conspiracy of nobles fed up with his reforms.

- **James II** (1437–1460): Son of James I, he inherited the throne aged 6. At 10 he witnessed revenge for his father's murder when leaders of the Douglas Clan were killed in front of him at the 'Black Dinner'. And he personally stabbed to death William, 8th Earl of Douglas, in 1452. He was killed by an exploding cannon at the siege of Roxburgh Castle, held by the English.

- James III (1460–1488): Son of James II, he was crowned at the age of 9. Marriage to Margaret, princess of Denmark, brought with it the islands of Orkney and Shetland. At war with his nobles and even his own son, he lost the Battle of Sauchieburn, and was killed, perhaps assassinated.

- James IV (1488–1513): Something of the Renaissance now reached Scotland, with the development of universities and the arrival of printing. James IV moved his court from Stirling to Edinburgh, which now became the capital. In 1503, James married Margaret Tudor, daughter of Henry VII. However, when Henry VIII started to pursue his military ambitions against France, Scotland's traditional allies, James felt obliged to invade England, but he was defeated and killed at the disastrous Battle of Flodden in 1513.

- James V (1513–1542): The son of James IV, he was just 17 months old when his father was killed. His mother, Margaret Tudor, then married into the despised Douglas family, and her husband imprisoned James until he escaped, aged 16. James, a Catholic, married the French Mary of Guise, and they had one surviving child, Mary, who became Queen of Scots. After defeat by the English, James suffered a nervous breakdown and died six days after Mary was born.

Mary, Queen of Scots: 1542-1567

Mary was crowned at Stirling Castle as a baby of 9 months. Her mother, Mary of Guise, acted as regent, and brought her up a Catholic. Henry VIII of England wanted her to marry his own infant son, but he was turned down and in 1548 Mary was packed off to France for her own safety. Mary of Guise died in 1554, after defeat by Protestant forces. Mary stayed in France and in 1558, aged 15, she married Francis, the Dauphin (heir to the French throne). She duly became Queen of France in 1559, but Francis died within a year. Widowed aged just 18, Mary returned to Scotland, where she faced increasingly angry opposition from Protestants: in 1560, the Scottish parliament had voted to make Scotland a Protestant nation.

In 1565, she married the unpleasant Henry Stewart, Lord Darnley. A seethingly jealous man, in 1566 Darnley ordered the murder of Mary's Italian secretary David Rizzio. Three months later, Mary gave birth to Darnley's son, James. The following year, Darnley was strangled and his house blown up, perhaps on the orders of James Hepburn, Earl of Bothwell – who then married Mary. The Scottish nobles were disgusted, and in 1567 they forced Mary to abdicate in favour of her one-year-old son James, who became James VI. Bothwell ran off to Denmark, and died insane in 1578. Mary sought refuge in England.

Queen Elizabeth kept Mary captive, mainly at Sheffield Castle, for 18 years (they never actually met). There were constant rumours that Mary was plotting against her. Eventually, in 1586, letters written by Mary linked her to the Babington Plot to murder Elizabeth. She was tried for treason and beheaded in the great hall of Fotheringhay Castle, Northamptonshire, in 1587.

Elizabeth claimed that she had tried to rescind the order of execution, and that she deeply regretted her death – but not everyone was convinced by her show of grief.

'You will do me great good in withdrawing me from this world out of which I am very glad to go.'

Mary, Queen of Scots, speaking the day before her execution.

**James VI of Scotland: 1567–1625
= James I of England: 1603–1625**

Crowned as a baby, James started to take control of Scotland from the age of 16. He had been brought up to hold a low opinion of his mother, and did little to intervene in her fate; rather, he maintained cordial relations with Elizabeth I. When Elizabeth I died in 1603, he was the next in line to the English throne through descent from Henry VII, his great-great-grandfather. He set off for London,

James VI and the witches

On returning from Denmark with his young bride, Anne of Denmark, in 1590, James was nearly shipwrecked in a storm. James blamed witches, and women were arrested and tried, accused of roasting wax images of the king, and of throwing a bewitched cat into the sea. Witch trials were common at this time, but these ones caused a sensation and a public mood of hysteria. James became obsessed with witchcraft and in 1597 wrote and published *Daemonologie*, a book linking witches to devil worship.

returning only once to Scotland, in 1617. He sent regular written instructions to the Scottish parliament, so he claimed that he ruled Scotland 'by a pen'.

A passion for golf

Scotland is called the 'home of golf'. It was such a popular game that James II – the spoilsport – tried to ban it, along with football. But this royal disapproval eventually evaporated, and a series of Scottish monarchs became avid enthusiasts, including James V, Mary Queen of Scots, James VI, Charles I, Charles II, James II and Bonnie Prince Charlie.

The Scottish Saltire

The flag of Scotland shows a white 'X' on a blue background. This is the cross of St Andrew, patron saint of Scotland, who supposedly chose to be martyred on a cross of this shape because he felt unworthy to use the same-shaped cross as Christ. St Andrew's cross had been a Scottish symbol for centuries, and is known to have been used for the flag of Scotland since the 1540s.

List of Stuart kings and queens of England and Scotland
1603–1649 and 1660–1714

James I, 1603–1625: son of Mary, Queen of Scots

Charles I, 1625–1649: son of James I

The Commonwealth, 1649–1660: no reigning monarch

Charles II, 1660–1685: son of Charles I

James II, 1685–1688: son of Charles I

William III, 1688–1702: grandson of Charles I, and **Mary II,** 1688–1694: daughter of James II

Anne, 1702–1714: daughter of James II

James the First and Sixth*, that's me – king of England *and* Scotland.

* James I of England, James VI of Scotland

CHAPTER TEN

THE STUARTS

Mary, Queen of Scots, cousin of Elizabeth I, had been second in line to the English throne. Elizabeth had her executed, but herself died without an heir – which made James, the son of Mary, Queen of Scots (and her husband Henry Stewart), next in line. It was Mary who changed the spelling of the family name to a French form, Stuart. When Elizabeth I died, James had already been King of Scotland for 35 years – and he was still only 36. Now he became the first king to wear both the crowns. The English public approved, but in the background lay a conflict that was not yet settled: Catholic vs. Protestant.

James I: 1603–1625

London offered a far more exciting social scene than Scotland, and James took to it with relish. He loved extravagant gestures, dressing in the finery inherited from the Elizabethan age. He commissioned the architect Inigo Jones to design two buildings in the fashionable Palladian classical style: the Banqueting Hall in Whitehall, and the Queen's House, Greenwich, for his wife Anne of Denmark. He sponsored an English translation of the Bible – the King James Bible. But he made enemies too, by showing too much favouritism to courtiers such as Robert Carr, Earl of Somerset, and George Villiers, Duke of Buckingham. 'The wisest fool in Christendom' is how the French ambassador described him.

Anti-smoking campaigner

James I had an obsession about witches, and he had an obsession about smoking – a new habit from North America, supposedly popularised by Sir Walter Raleigh. 'A custome loathsome to the eye, hateful to the nose, harmful to the brain, dangerous to the lungs,' he wrote in a book on the subject.

The Gunpowder Plot

A group of Roman Catholics plotted to blow up the Houses of Parliament while the King was visiting, using 36 barrels of gunpowder hidden in the cellar. It was to be the opening salvo of an ambitious plot to replace James with a Catholic monarch. An intercepted letter from the leader, Robert Catesby, to a Catholic lord, unmasked the plot and led to the discovery of the gunpowder on 5 November, along with one of the plotters, Guy Fawkes. He and other members of the plot were rounded up, tortured and executed. This event is still celebrated each year on 5 November with fireworks and the burning of a replica 'Guy' on bonfires.

Remember, remember the fifth of November,
gunpowder, treason and plot,
I see no reason why gunpowder treason
should ever be forgot.
Guy Fawkes, Guy Fawkes,
'twas his intent
to blow up the King and the Parliament.
Threescore barrels of powder below,
Poor old England to overthrow:
By God's providence he was catch'd
With a dark lantern and burning match.
Holloa boys, holloa boys, make the bells ring.
Holloa boys, holloa boys, God save the King!
Hip hip hoorah!

(Traditional nursery rhyme)

Charles I: 1625–1649

He may have been only 1.6 m (5 ft 4 in) tall, but Charles had very grand ideas about himself. He married a witty and vivacious French princess, Henrietta Maria. Charles relied on his chosen advisors, bypassing Parliament, and in 1642, when he demanded the arrest of five members of Parliament and their supporters, civil war broke out. After five years, Charles I was imprisoned, and finally beheaded on a scaffold erected outside the Banqueting Hall in Whitehall, London.

The Divine Right of Kings

'A king cannot be tried by any superior jurisdiction on earth,' declared Charles at his trial. Like his father, James I, and like Louis XIV in France (reigned 1643–1715), Charles believed that he had been chosen by God to rule, and only God could judge him. He was, effectively, above the law. This centuries-old idea became a hotly debated issue in Stuart times when it was questioned by Protestants. In British history, the concept effectively died with Charles, although the motto 'Dieu et mon droit' ('God and my right') remains part of the royal coat of arms.

Civil War:
Roundheads vs. Cavaliers

On one side were the supporters of the King: they had long hair, wore big feathered hats and fancy clothes, and were nicknamed the Cavaliers. Ranged against them were supporters of Parliament, led by their general, Oliver Cromwell; many of these were Puritans with shaven heads: they were nicknamed Roundheads. Highlights included:

1642: Battle of Edgehill, Warwickshire. Inconclusive.

1644: Battle of Marston Moor, near York. The bloodiest battle of the war, ending in victory for the Parliamentarians.

1645: Battle of Naseby, Northamptonshire. Victory for the Parliamentarians.

1646: Charles I seeks protection of the Scottish Presbyterian army in Nottinghamshire, but is handed over to the Parliamentarians.

1649: Execution of Charles I. His son, also called Charles, tries to reclaim the throne, supported by Scots who recognise him as King of Scotland.

1650: Battle of Dunbar, Scotland. Victory for the Parliamentarians.

1651: Charles II is crowned King of Scotland in Scone, the last king to be crowned on Scottish soil.

1651: Battle of Worcester. Victory for the Parliamentarians; Charles II escapes by hiding in an oak tree, then flees into exile.

Oliver Cromwell and the Commonwealth: 1649–1660

Oliver Cromwell (1599–1658), a small landowner from Huntingdon and a Member of Parliament, rose to prominence at the start of the Civil War. After the execution of Charles I, the country was ruled as a republic called the Commonwealth, with Oliver Cromwell in charge as the 'Lord Protector'. In 1657 Parliament asked him to be king, but he refused. When he died the following year, his son Richard took over as Lord Protector, but 'Tumbledown Dick' was not a gifted leader, and soon stood down. People asked: if leadership was to pass from father to son, why not just have a king?

Cromwell in Ireland

During the 16th and early 17th centuries the lands of Irish Catholics had been forcibly taken from them and given to Protestant settlers from England and Scotland, in a process called 'plantation'. In 1641, Roman Catholics in Ireland rebelled, and they established their own government called the Confederation of Kilkenny. Eight years later,

Cromwell arrived to take cruel revenge: over the next four years he and his New Model Army brought utter destruction to Ireland. Many people were massacred or deported; Churches were sacked. Land was distributed among the Protestant victors.

Executing a dead body

Oliver Cromwell was originally buried in Westminster Abbey, the traditional resting place of kings. The year after the Restoration of the monarchy, on 30 January (the annversary of Charles I's execution), fanatics tore up his grave and then put his body through the process of execution. They hanged it in chains at Tyburn, a place of public execution in London, then the head was put on a pole outside Westminster Hall, where it remained for almost 14 years. After passing through the hands of various owners, in 1960 the head was finally buried in Sidney Sussex College, Cambridge (where Cromwell had been a student).

The Plague and the Great fire

The early years of Charles II's reign were marked by two major disasters. First, in 1665, came the Great Plague, a foul disease spread by the fleas of rats. Some 100,000 people died. Then came the Great Fire, in 1666: it started in a bakery in Pudding Lane and spread rapidly. Official records suggest that very few people died, but much of London was destroyed. Sir Christopher Wren was put in charge of rebuilding London, and designed the new St Paul's Cathedral and 52 other churches.

Charles II: 1660–1685

The eldest son of Charles I, meanwhile, had been living extravagantly in France and the Spanish Netherlands (Belgium). Now he saw his opportunity. He wrote to the English Parliament, negotiated the terms of the 'Restoration', and returned to London in triumph to become King Charles II. The 'Merry Monarch' set the tone for an era of lavish, swaggering style. Charles had plenty of mistresses and numerous illegitimate children, but none by his wife, the Portuguese princess Catherine of Braganza. So the heir to the throne was Charles's brother James – a Roman Catholic.

'Here lies our mutton-eating King,
Whose word no man relies on;
Who never said a foolish thing,
Nor ever did a wise one.'

John Wilmot, 2nd Earl of Rochester,
on King Charles II

Grisly deaths

Charles II was fascinated by chemistry, and had a laboratory at Whitehall. He believed that mercury was a powerful medicine – in fact it is a poison. He was taken ill on 2 February 1685, with violent fits. He was bled by his physicians (excess blood was thought to cause disease) for four days, and given medicine which included crushed human skull. But ultimately he probably died of mercury poisoning. Charles II was not the first king, nor the last, to endure a painful or violent death. Here are some of the more famous ones:

Edmund I, a Saxon king, was stabbed to death by a robber in a brawl.

William I, the Conqueror, was fatally injured when his horse stumbled and threw him onto the pommel of his saddle. He died from internal injuries some weeks later.

William II, 'Rufus', was killed by an arrow in the New Forest in mysterious circumstances.

Richard I, 'The Lionheart', was hit in the shoulder by a shot from a crossbow. The bolt was clumsily removed, the wound became infected with gangrene, and he died 12 days later.

Edward II was murdered when he was a prisoner in Berkeley Castle, apparently by having a red-hot poker shoved up his behind through a horn – an agonizing death, but one that also leaves no obvious external marks.

Edward V, one of the Princes in the Tower, was probably murdered at the age of 12, in 1483.

James II of Scotland was killed by an exploding cannon at the siege of Roxburgh Castle.

Richard III was killed at the battle of Bosworth Field, in 1485.

James III of Scotland – the story goes – was knifed by an assassin disguised as a priest, after losing the Battle of Sauchieburn.

Mary, Queen of Scots was beheaded at Fotheringhay Castle. She carried a lapdog under her skirt, so her body appeared to keep moving after her death.

George II died on the toilet, after eating an excessive amount of chocolate and suffering a heart attack.

James II: 1685–1688

A fervent Catholic, 'Dismal Jimmy' appointed his Catholic friends to key positions, and clashed with Parliament. Through his earlier marriage to Anne Hyde, a Protestant, he had two daughters, Mary and Anne; but Anne Hyde had died in 1671. He then married a Catholic Italian princess, Mary of Modena, and they had a son, James. The prospect of a Catholic heir alarmed Parliament. So they approached Mary, daughter of James and Anne Hyde, who was married to the Protestant Dutch prince, William of Orange – and asked them to take over. James quickly abandoned the throne and was ushered away to France.

The Monmouth Rebellion

James II faced opposition from the moment he became king. In 1685 the Duke of Monmouth, the eldest illegitimate son of Charles II, returned from exile in Holland to lead a rebellion. But he was roundly defeated at the Battle of Sedgemoor. Monmouth's supporters were condemned to be hanged, flogged or deported by Judge Jeffreys at the notoriously harsh 'Bloody Assizes'. As for Monmouth, it took some six blows of the axe to complete his execution on Tower Hill.

The Maundy ceremony

The Thursday before Easter is called Maundy Thursday. Since the 13th century, the king of England had washed the feet of poor people, to demonstrate his humility, in the same way as Christ had washed the feet of his Disciples. But James II thought he was far too grand to do this, and gave out coins to the poor instead. That tradition has remained to this day: on Maundy Thursday the Queen gives out specially minted coins to selected elderly members of the public. The number of recipients corresponds to the sovereign's age.

A Victorian Maundy ceremony

William III (1688–1702) and Mary II (1688–1694)

So William of Orange, ruler of Holland (and the part of France called Orange), arrived in the little port of Brixham in Devon on 15 November 1688 and began his march on London. He encountered very little opposition, and James fled without a fight. This was the 'Glorious Revolution': England now had a King and a Queen, who ruled jointly, as equals. Mary died of smallpox in 1694, aged 32, after which William ruled alone.

The Battle of the Boyne

James II decided that he would try to win back the throne of England through Ireland, where he still had many supporters among its Catholic population. So in 1690 he arrived in Ireland and assembled an army. William brought over an army to repel him, and they clashed by the River Boyne near Drogheda. William won, and eventually took control of Ireland. To this day, Ireland remains divided along religious grounds, and some Protestants call themselves Orangemen in honour of William of Orange. James II died in France in 1701.

The massacre at Glencoe

Many Scots did not approve of the accession of William and Mary, and remained loyal to the Stuart line of kings. William began a campaign to win over the clans, requiring them one by one to swear an oath of allegiance. In the bitter winter of 1692, the Macdonalds of Glencoe came late to one such meeting. To teach them a lesson, soldiers loyal to William from the Campbell clan (old enemies of the Macdonalds) entered the Valley of Glencoe, where the Macdonalds gave them shelter. Then one morning the soldiers turned on the Macdonalds, forced them into the snow and killed the chief, his wife and 37 clansmen.

Anne: 1702–1714

William and Mary had no children, so next in line was Anne, Mary's sister. Aged 37 when she came to the throne, she ruled through a period of great military success in Europe, where John Churchill, 1st Duke of Marlborough, scored famous victories against the French, such as the Battle of Blenheim in 1704. Anne was married to Prince George of Denmark; they had 17 children, but these all died in childhood. In her last years Anne became seriously ill, and so fat and lame she could barely leave Kensington Palace.

The Act of Union

Until 1707, England and Scotland had separate parliaments. But under the Act of Union, government was brought under one Parliament, in London. The separate Kingdoms of Scotland and England now formed Great Britain. Anne therefore became the first sovereign of Great Britain (her predecessors had been sovereigns of England and Scotland). England achieved agreement from Scotland after a long political tussle, and by offering huge inducements of money, trading advantages, jobs, honours and titles.

The Royal Touch

Many people believed that kings and queens were chosen by God, and so they had divine powers – and the power to cure the sick through the 'Royal Touch'. Elizabeth I believed in these powers, and Charles II is said to have touched 92,000 people during his lifetime. Anne maintained this tradition, but to no visible effect, and after she died, the practice was abandoned.

The Act of Settlement

Anne's longest-surviving child, James, had died at the age of 11 in 1700, before she came to the throne. Parliament decided, therefore, to organise her successor, and to ensure that the Roman Catholic Stuarts could never inherit the throne. So in 1701 the Act of Settlement was passed, stating that, after Anne, the crown would pass to the granddaughter of James I, the Electress Sophia of Hanover (in Germany), or her Protestant heirs. This rule still applies: heirs to the British throne must be members of the Church of England, and cannot marry a Roman Catholic.

List of Hanoverian kings and queens

1714 –1901

George I, 1714–1727: great-grandson of James I
George II, 1727–1760: son of George I
George III, 1760–1820: grandson of George II
George IV, 1820–1830: son of George III
William IV, 1830–1837: son of George III
Victoria, 1837–1901: granddaughter of George III

George III

When George III's mental health declined, his son George took on the role of Prince Regent.

George IV as Prince Regent

THE HANOVERIANS

So, as planned, when Queen Anne died, the throne passed to the Protestant line of the granddaughter of James I, the German Electress Sophia of Hanover. She had actually died two months before Anne, so the succession passed to her eldest son, George. He spoke little English, and had never set foot in Britain in all his 54 years. He had divorced his German wife Sophia Dorothea of Brunswick and Lunenburg, and kept her imprisoned in Germany. A strange choice for King, you might think, but it was accepted well enough in England. So began the rule of the House of Hanover, which was to last nearly 200 years.

George I: 1714–1727 – 'German George'
These were peaceful times: Britain prospered, reaping the benefits of its growing empire. Parliament grew stronger, partly because George spent much of his time in Germany. He left Britain in the control of the head of government in Parliament. From 1721 on, this was Sir Robert Walpole, who became the first politician to hold the title of Prime Minister. George I was a brute, and his son George II hated him. He died, aged 66, in his coach on his way back to Germany.

George II: 1727–1760 – 'Soldier George'
George II's reign coincided with the complicated War of Austrian Succession (1740–1748). In 1743, at the Battle of Dettingen in Germany, he became the last British monarch personally to lead his troops in battle, scoring a victory over the French. During his reign Britain also secured territory in India and Canada, notably through General James Wolfe in Quebec. George was dull and bad-tempered, in contrast to his vivacious German wife, Caroline of Brandenburg-Ansbach; they had eight children. George died aged 76.

The Jacobite risings

James II's son, James Edward Stuart, believed he had a stronger claim to the English throne than George I – not without reason. He had plenty of supporters, especially among Catholics. They became known as 'Jacobites', from Jacobus, the Latin version of James. He made a weak attempt to invade England in 1715 before retreating, then lived to the age of 78, mainly in Rome. He became known as the 'Old Pretender', from the old use of the word *pretend* meaning 'to claim'.

The 'Young Pretender' was his 24-year-old son Charles Edward Stuart, known as 'Bonnie Prince Charlie'. In 1745, Charles launched a Jacobite rebellion from Scotland. He captured Edinburgh, won the Battle of Prestonpans, and then headed south, getting to within 130 miles (210 km) of London, before retreating. Back in Scotland, the rebels were massacred in 1746 at the Battle of Culloden, near Inverness. Bonnie Prince Charlie fled 'over the sea to Skye' (as the 'Skye Boat Song' recalls) disguised as a maid. From there he returned to France. He died in Rome in 1788, aged 67.

'Off with their heads!'

In 1789, the French Revolution overthrew the monarchy, and King Louis XVI and his queen Marie Antoinette were imprisoned. In 1793 they were executed by guillotine. Between 16,000 and 40,000 people suffered the same fate; many of them members of the aristocracy who were connected to, or supported, the monarchy. France was in chaos.

Britain looked on nervously: it had its own revolutionaries. There was seething discontent. Handbills were pasted up in various parts of the country bearing slogans like: 'God save the poor and down with George III'. Rebels were arrested and harshly treated. It is said that, by 1801, the people might even have welcomed the French Revolutionary Army as liberators. Soon, however, the war with Napoleon provided a new focus for loyalty and new heroes like Nelson and Wellington – and the British monarchy survived.

Britain escaped revolution partly because it was a fairer place, with Parliament now holding much of the power of decision-making. Above all though, George III was popular – or at least popular enough. By contrast, Louis XVI and especially his wife, Marie Antoinette, were deeply unpopular, and the focus of fevered hatred.

George III: 1760–1820 – 'Farmer George'

George III, the grandson of George II, was the first Hanoverian king to seem almost English: he had been raised in England, spoke English (with a German accent) and enjoyed the countryside so much he was called 'Farmer George'. By the Act of Union, passed by the Parliament of Ireland in 1800, he was the first King of the United Kingdom and Ireland. Like his predecessors, he married a German, Charlotte Sophia of Mecklenburg-Strelitz, and they produced a large and close-knit family, with 15 children. Unfortunately, George III suffered from mental illness, and after 1811 his son, also called George, took over and reigned in his place as the Prince Regent.

The Union Jack

In 1603, when James I brought together the thrones of England and Scotland, a flag was devised that joined the red cross of St George (patron saint of England) with the white X-shaped cross or saltire of St Andrew (for Scotland). In 1801 Ireland joined the union and so the red saltire of St Patrick (for Ireland) was added. The resulting design was known as the Union Flag or 'Union Jack'.

Losing America

In the 150 years since the first English settlements on the east coast of North America, the 13 British colonies had prospered. The inhabitants did not much like being ruled by distant England, and paying high taxes to London. In 1773, colonists in Boston rebelled against a tax on tea by throwing chests of tea from a ship into the harbour. This 'Boston Tea Party' led to the Declaration of Independence in 1776, and the War of Independence. Britain lost one of its most valuable colonial possessions.

The 'madness' of George III

After the age of about 50, George III suffered from bouts of mental illness. This was probably caused by a disease of the blood called porphyria, which made him delusional. He would talk non-stop, ending all his sentences with the word 'peacock'; he wandered about Windsor Castle in a battered old dressing gown; and mistook a tree for the King of Prussia. He died aged 82, after a decade of unrelieved 'madness'.

War with Napoleon

After the French Revolution, a new and ambitious leader of France emerged from the chaos. He was an army officer from Corsica called Napoleon Bonaparte. His rise to glory began when he successfully led armies against the enemies of France, then he began invading countries right across Europe, from Spain to Russia. Britain was under threat, and not very well led by its mentally ill king and lazy, party-loving Prince Regent. But it had superb military forces. Under Lord Nelson, Britain's navy scored a classic victory at the Battle of Trafalgar, off the coast of Spain, in 1805. Nelson lost his life in the battle, turning him from a celebrity to a national hero of cult status. And the great general the Duke of Wellington finally finished Napoleon off at the Battle of Waterloo, Belgium, in 1815. The war had lasted some 20 years, covering much of the final years of George III's long reign.

Napoleon
Bonaparte
(1769–1821)

The Prince Regent (1811–1820)

George III's mental state had deteriorated so far by 1811 that he could no longer reign, so his son George, aged 49, took over as Prince Regent. This was an era in which new industrial wealth and high profits from trade were lavishly spent on high fashion, dinners and elegant homes. 'The Regency Period' has a refined and delicate ring to it, but the Prince ('Prinny') himself – at the heart of this social whirl – was a gross and relentless party animal.

Rude and crude

A new kind of popular art emerged in Georgian times: cartoonists made prints poking fun at the excesses of politicians, doctors, generals, the nobility, the new industrial tycoons – and the royal family. The most famous of the cartoonists were Thomas Rowlandson (1756–1817) and James Gillray (1757–1815), who were merciless in their depictions of high society. The overweight Prince Regent in particular came in for stinging attack, but there was nothing he could do about it: the cartoons were too popular, and to stop them would have caused rebellion.

Brighton Pavilion

The Prince Regent's most extravagant project was his fantasy palace in Brighton, the newly fashionable seaside resort. Designed by the highly respected architect John Nash, and built between 1815 and 1822, it is a fabulous concoction of exotic styles: Moghul-Indian, Islamic, Egyptian, Chinese – and French.

George IV: 1820–1830

Eventually George III died, after a reign of 59 years. The Prince Regent, now aged 57, at last became king. By this time he was immensely fat and unwell, and spent a large part of the day in bed. Things moved ahead without him. Stephenson built the first steam railway to carry passengers, and the police force was founded by Sir Robert Peel. Nonetheless, when George IV died, *The Times* reported: 'Never was an individual less regretted by his fellow creatures than this deceased King.'

Caroline of Brunswick

In 1785, when he was 22, the future George IV secretly married his mistress, a Catholic widow called Maria Fitzherbert. This outraged his father, and Parliament declared the marriage invalid. In 1795, he was persuaded to marry his German cousin Caroline of Brunswick. He detested her, and they spent only two nights together – but this produced a daughter, Charlotte. Caroline went to live in Italy. When the Prince Regent became king, however, she returned to take up her place as queen; but she was locked out of the coronation ceremony at Westminster Abbey. Three weeks later, she died.

The king's breakfast

The Prince Regent was a glutton, and grew so fat he was nicknamed 'The Prince of Whales'. His breakfast might typically consist of:

- An aperitif of laudanum (a poppy-based drug)
- A beef pie made with 5–6 steaks and 2–3 pigeons
- Champagne, port, moselle (white wine) and claret (red wine)

William IV: 1830–1837

George IV had one daughter with Caroline of Brunswick: Charlotte. She married the German Prince Leopold of Saxe-Coburg, but died in childbirth in 1817. So the new heir to the throne was George's brother William. He was 64 when he became king; he had been in the navy, so he was called 'The Sailor King'. William ('Silly Billy') was unconventional, to say the least; he wore peculiar clothes and liked to chat to complete strangers in the street. He had 10 children by his mistress, Dorothea Bland, but there were no surviving children from his marriage to the German Princess Adelaide of Saxe-Meiningen.

Royal mistresses

While still a prince, William IV lived openly for 20 years with his mistress, the actress Dorothea Bland (stage name 'Mrs Jordan'), and their 10 children. Royal mistresses were usually treated with a fair amount of respect, and some were given noble ranks. Sons were often acknowledged by the name FitzRoy (*fils du roi*, 'son of the king').

Here are a few of them:

Rosamund Clifford (before 1150–c.1176): mistress of Henry II. 'Fair Rosamund' was a celebrated beauty, who stayed with Henry from about 1166 to 1174, and much to the fury of his wife, Eleanor of Aquitaine. It is not clear whether they had children.

Bessie Blount (c.1502–1539/40): mistress of Henry VIII. A maid-of-honour to Catherine of Aragon, she became Henry's mistress from about 1514 (he was about 23, she was perhaps 13) until about 1522. In 1519 she gave birth to a son, named Henry FitzRoy, later Duke of Richmond and Somerset; he died in 1536.

Nell Gwyn (1650–1687): mistress of Charles II (one of many). An actress, she was Charles's mistress from 1668 until his death in 1685, and they had two sons. The elder, Charles, became the first Duke of St Albans. Nell was a popular folk heroine in her day.

Louise de Kérouaille (1649–1734): another mistress of Charles II. From a noble family of Brittany, she was his mistress from about 1670 until Charles's death. She was given the titles Baroness Petersfield, Countess of Fareham and Duchess of Portsmouth. Louise's descendants include: Diana, Princess of Wales; Camilla, Duchess of Cornwall; and Sarah, Duchess of York.

Melusine von der Schulenburg (1667–1743): mistress of George I. Known as 'The Maypole', because she was so thin, she became Duchess of Kendal, Countess of Feversham and Baroness Glastonbury.

Sophia von Kielmansegg (1675–1725): George I's other mistress. Known as 'The Elephant' because she was short and fat, she became the Countess of Darlington.

Lillie Langtry (1853–1929): mistress to the future Edward VII (one of many). A famous beauty, she had an affair with Edward that lasted from 1877 to 1880, after which she became a well-known actress.

Victoria: 1837–1901

When William IV died, the next in line was Princess Victoria, a young woman of 18 – Wiliam's niece, the daughter of his younger brother Edward Augustus and Victoria of Saxe-Coburg-Saalfeld. Despite her fame as one of Britain's greatest monarchs, Victoria was only 5 ft (1.52 m) tall. She took her constitutional responsibilities seriously. Her prolonged period of mourning for her husband after 1861 turned her into a black-clothed recluse, but because of her constancy and diligence her reign ended with great public respect and affection.

Prince Consort

Victoria was a passionate woman, and when she was 20 years old she fell passionately in love with her German cousin Albert, Duke of Saxony and Prince of Saxe-Coburg-Gotha. They were married in 1840. Deeply devoted to each other, they produced nine children. Albert was hardworking and serious, a scientist thrilled by the possibilities of modern technology. But Britain never warmed to him, and Parliament refused to give him a noble title. He remained HRH Prince Albert until 1857, when Victoria herself gave him the title 'Prince Consort'.

'We are not amused'

This is the most famous quotation attached to Queen Victoria. But no-one knows quite when she said it, or even whether she said it at all. It seems to have stuck because it somehow symbolises the seriousness with which Victoria undertook her duties, and her grim decades of unsmiling mourning after the death of her beloved Prince Albert.

VICTORIA QUEEN AND EMPRESS ✤ COMFORTER OF THE AFFLICTED ✤

It was a truly *awful* puppet show, though.

Victoria's royal palaces

Buckingham Palace: Originally built in 1705, it became the principal London residence of Queen Victoria after 1837, when she transferred from St James's Palace.

Kensington Palace: Designed by Sir Christopher Wren for William and Mary, it opened in 1689 at a time when Kensington was a village outside London. It was the main royal residence until the death of George II in 1760. More recently, it has been the home of Princess Margaret and of Diana, Princess of Wales.

St James's Palace: Originally built for Henry VIII in 1536.

Windsor Castle: This mighty Norman fortress, by the River Thames and to the west of London, was transformed in stages over the years, and remains a royal residence today. A fire in 1992 caused extensive damage to the grand receptions rooms, but they have since been restored.

Frogmore House: located in the Home Park of Windsor Castle, it has served as the country retreat of various monarchs since the 17th century. It was a favourite residence of Queen Victoria; the gardens contain the mausoleum where Prince Albert and later Victoria herself were buried.

Osborne House: This delightful pala[...]
Isle of Wight was built for Queen Vic[...]
an Italian villa style in 1845–1851. Now u[...]
the care of English Heritage and open to [...]
public, it offers a unique insight into the family
life of Queen Victoria.

Palace of Holyroodhouse, Edinburgh: Built
originally as a monastery in 1128, it was the
home of Scottish monarchs, including Mary,
Queen of Scots, from 1560 to 1567. It remains
the Queen's official residence in Scotland.

Brighton Pavilion: Queen Victoria disliked
the Prince Regent's fantasy palace, and it was
sold to the town of Brighton in 1850.

Kew Palace: This beautiful little palace in
Richmond (west of London) was a residence of
George III. Queen Victoria gave the gardens to
the nation, and they became the famous Royal
Botanic Gardens.

Balmoral: A neo-baronial castle in the
Highlands of Scotland, on the River Dee,
Aberdeenshire, it sits on an estate bought by
Victoria and Albert in 1852, and was completed
in 1856. It remains a royal residence
and is much cherished as a
quiet family retreat.

The Great Exhibition

...ain led the Industrial Revolution. Powered ...rst by water, then by steam engines, the new factories had cranked up mass production in just about every field of commercial activity. By the mid-19th century there was a strong feeling that there were no limits to what industry and technology combined might achieve, to the great benefit of humankind.

To celebrate this, and Britain's leading role in industrial development, London hosted the Great Exhibition in 1851. The first international exhibition of its kind, it took place in a ground-breaking temporary building erected in Hyde Park and built almost entirely of glass and steel: the 'Crystal Palace'.

Prince Albert took a leading role in organising the Great Exhibition. Queen Victoria opened it on 1 May 1851, and the royal couple visited it 34 times. More than six million visitors came – many by the new method of public transport, the train – to admire 100,000 exhibits from around the world, including steam engines, mass-produced sculptures, glass fountains, weird inventions such as the 300-blade pocket-knife, and the priceless Koh-i-Noor Diamond (now a part of the Crown Jewels).

The achievements of the Victorian age

In the 63 years of Queen Victoria's reign, Britain was transformed by rapid developments in technology. Victoria and Albert themselves were thrilled by photography and were avid enthusiasts of modern invention, installing the latest equipment and gadgets in their houses. Over the course of Victoria's reign Britain went:

- From horses and carriages to a complete railway network and the motor car
- From sailing ships to steamships
- From candles, oil lamps and gas street lamps to electric lighting
- From painting to photography and cine films
- From quill and paper to typewriters
- From hand-stitching to the sewing machine
- From written messages to the telephone
- From visual telegraphy to Morse code and radio
- From concerts to recorded sound
- From chamber pots to flushing toilets.

The death of Prince Albert

During the cold winter of 1861 Albert caught typhoid, probably from faulty drains at Windsor Castle. He died at the age of 42. Queen Victoria was devastated. She withdrew from public life, dressed in black; still in her early forties, she became a reclusive widow, and was rarely seen in public for more than 15 years. Meanwhile she had the magnificent Albert Memorial built in his honour in Hyde Park, and the Albert Hall opposite. Many people began to grow impatient with her absence from public life.

After Albert's death, Queen Victoria became very close to a loyal Scottish servant called John Brown. He organised her life for her, and clearly brought her great comfort. In 1862 a man with a gun approached the Queen's carriage outside Buckingham Palace, and John Brown wrestled him to the ground – an act which Victoria claimed had saved her life. When John Brown died in 1883, she was bereft. It has never been clear quite what the relationship was, but when Victoria died, on her instructions a lock of his hair was placed in her coffin.

Royal Warrants

Royal Warrants have been handed out suppliers of goods and services to the royal family since the days of Henry II. This is a great badge of honour for the recipients, who can use the royal coat of arms, and the words 'By appointment to...', to announce that they supply members of the royal family.

Queen Victoria raised the profile of Royal Warrants by issuing some 2,000 of them. The tradition continues today: the Queen, the Duke of Edinburgh and Prince Charles have all issued Royal Warrants to chosen suppliers who have to have a record of at least five years of service to them. Today there are some 800 Royal Warrant holders in Britain. A Royal Warrant expires on the death of the person who issued it, and can be cancelled at any time. Royal Warrants for suppliers of cigarettes, for instance, were withdrawn in 1999.

The British Empire

The Empire on which the sun never sets' was the proud boast, when Britain controlled overseas territories that stretched right around the globe. They included India, Canada, Australia, New Zealand – 400 million people, one fifth of the world, in territories marked in pink on school atlas maps. Britain grew rich on protected trade and access to raw materials.

The British Empire was nearing its peak during the reign of Queen Victoria. This was a period when European nations were grabbing land all around the world, particularly in Africa. Queen Victoria took a great interest in these developments. They were not always positive: although the British liked to think they were spreading the benefits of justice, education, trade and industrial production, empire-building often required the assertion of power backed by brutal military action.

The pursuit of empire and global politics led to ugly and bloody confrontations, such as the Opium Wars in China (1839–1842 and 1856–1860), the Crimean War (1853–6), the Indian Mutiny (1857), the Zulu War (1879), and the Boer War (1899–1902) in South Africa. Victoria followed all of these in close detail, feeling every setback as a personal loss. The Victoria Cross, still the highest award for military bravery, was first awarded in 1856, during the Crimean War.

Empress of India

After Albert's death, when the Queen hid away from public view, she continued to work on state affairs, ably assisted by two great, rival Prime Ministers, Benjamin Disraeli and William Gladstone. It was Disraeli who, in 1876, came up with the idea to make Queen Victoria 'Empress of India', and this new honour and responsibility helped to bring her back into public life. Despite the title, she never actually visited India, but she took a close interest in this important colonial possession. She employed Indian staff and even learnt Hindi and Punjabi.

The Jubilees

In 1887 Britain celebrated Queen Victoria's Golden Jubilee, marking her 50th year on the throne. A banquet was held in London for 50 European kings and princes, and the next day a huge procession was greeted with popular acclaim. In 1897, her 60th year on the throne – now the longest reign in British history – was marked her Diamond Jubilee, which was elevated into a festival of the British Empire, attended by leaders of all the colonies and dominions.

The funeral of Queen Victoria

Queen Victoria died on 22 January 1901 at Osborne House, at the age of 81, surrounded by family. The whole nation went into mourning. Her funeral was more magnificent and elaborate than any before, witnessed by vast and silent crowds all along the route – from the Isle of Wight by boat and train, through the streets of London and finally to her last resting place beside Prince Albert at the Royal Mausoleum at Frogmore, Windsor.

'Grandmother of Europe'

Through her 9 children and 42 grandchildren, their marriages and family connections, Queen Victoria became the hub of a power network that spread across Europe.

Her own nine children were:

- **Princess Victoria** (1840–1901), mar[...] Frederick III, Emperor of Germany, and beca[...] the mother of Kaiser Wilhelm II

- **Prince Albert Edward** ('Bertie'; 1841–1910), Prince of Wales, the future King Edward VII

- **Princess Alice** (1843–1878), married Louis IV, Grand Duke of Hesse

- **Prince Alfred** (1844–1900), Duke of Saxe-Coburg and Gotha and Duke of Edinburgh, Admiral of the Fleet, married Grand Duchess Maria Alexandrovna (daughter of Tsar Alexander II of Russia), father of Marie of Edinburgh, Queen of Romania

- **Princess Helena** (1846–1923), married Prince Christian of Schleswig-Holstein-Sonderburg-Augustenburg

- **Princess Louise** (1848–1939), married John Douglas Sutherland Campbell (1845–1914), 9th Duke of Argyll

- **Prince Arthur** (1850–1942), Duke of Connaught and Strathearn, married Princess Louise Margaret of Prussia

- **Prince Leopold** (1853–1884), Duke of Albany, married Princess Helena of Waldeck and Pyrmont

- **Princess Beatrice** (1857–1944), married Prince Henry of Battenberg, and was the mother of Victoria Eugenie, Queen of Spain.

SAXE-COBURG-GOTHA (1901–1910)

Edward VII, 1901–1910: son of Victoria

THE WINDSORS (1910–present)

George V, 1910–1936: son of Edward VII
Edward VIII, 1936: son of George V
George VI, 1936–1952: son of George V
Elizabeth II, 1952–present: daughter of
  George VI

The 1969
investiture
of Prince
Charles

CHAPTER TWELVE

SAXE~COBURG GOTHA & THE WINDSORS

W hen Queen Victoria died, she lay on her bed, supported on the arm of her grandson, Kaiser Wilhelm II of Germany. In just a few years he was to become Britain's No. 1 enemy, as Europe stumbled into the First World War. Edward VII was the only king to complete his reign as a member of the House of Saxe-Coburg-Gotha (named after Prince Albert's line). This same dynasty is the one that rules today, but in 1917, during the First World War, it changed its name to Windsor to mask its German origins.

VII: 1901–1910

...1 Albert Edward, the Prince of Wales, ...s just short of 60, a plump and pampered gentleman used to years of good living and fine food. Known as Bertie to his family, he took the name Edward VII at his coronation. He had been married to Princess Alexandra of Denmark since 1863; of their six children, four were still living. For a decade he presided over the 'Belle Epoque' of comfortable prosperity in Britain, which was enjoying the fruits of its Empire, its trade, industry and technology – motorcars, telephones, even aeroplanes after 1903. But beneath the glitter and pleasure of the Edwardian Era was also despair and utter poverty, even in the heart of London, the capital of the Empire.

A royal potato

King Edward potatoes are one of the best-known varieties of potato in Britain today. They were introduced in Lincolnshire in 1902, the year of the coronation of Edward VII, and so his name became forever attached to them.

154

'Good old Teddy'

'I never can, or shall, look at him without a shudder', said Queen Victoria, who thoroughly disapproved of her eldest son and his spoilt and immoral ways. Shooting, horse-racing, card-games, parties, drinking and smoking cigars were Edward's favourite pastimes – and pursuing a string of glamorous mistresses. But as king he buckled down and served with diligence and dignity.

George V

Queen Victoria

Edward VIII

Edward VII

1910–1936

Edward VII died his son took over, at age of 45, as George V. His reign was then overshadowed by the First World War. This coincided with the Russian Revolution of 1917, which saw the annihilation of the Tsar and his family – George's cousins. Closer to home, Ireland rebelled against British rule and became independent (except for Northern Ireland) in 1921, and Britain's economy sank into Depression and industrial turbulence. In these tough times, George V did much to sustain public spirits.

The lost Prince

The fifth child of George V, Prince John (1905–1919), suffered from epilepsy. Always fragile, he was kept out of public view, and lived mainly at a farm on the Sandringham Estate in Norfolk, in the care of a nanny. He suffered his first epileptic seizure when he was 4, and did not attend his father's coronation two years later. He died aged 13. It is a measure of the need of the royal family to maintain the appearance of perfection, that very little was known about him until the TV film *The Lost Prince* was first aired in 2003.

The first World War

The First World War (1914–1918) was European calamity in which 10 million people died. It was especially uncomfortable for the British royal family because the main enemy, Germany, was led by Kaiser Wilhelm II, a grandchild of Queen Victoria and a cousin of George V.

War had been brewing for many years, as Germany's ambitions to be an imperial nation, rivalling Britain, were fuelled by an arms race. The assassination of Archduke Franz Ferdinand, heir to the Austro-Hungarian Empire, in Sarajevo brought into play a series of treaties of alliance. When war was declared, many Britons rejoiced. But the armies soon reached stalemate in the trenches of Flanders in Belgium, and in northeastern France.

The royal family, soon to be rebranded Windsor, took a keen interest in the war, but mainly from the sidelines. George V had a particular interest in the navy that earned him the nickname 'The Sailor King'. Edward, the Prince of Wales, served in the army – but he was not allowed to become involved in frontline action, for fear that he would be killed or captured. His younger brother Prince Albert (the future George VI), however, was in the navy and, as a 20-year-old midshipman, took part in the Battle of Jutland, the biggest sea battle of the First World War, in 1916.

Edward VIII and Mrs Simp...

As Prince of Wales, George V's son Edward (called David by his family) was a popular public figure – partying with the glamorous, fashionable London set, but showing that he had 'the common touch' when dealing with ordinary working people.

But there was trouble ahead. By the time he became king, as Edward VIII, in 1936, he was in love with an American woman called Wallis Simpson – a divorcée soon to be divorced from her second husband. Parliament declared that marriage was impossible: either she went, or Edward would have to abdicate (give up the throne). He chose love and decided to marry. So Edward VIII reigned for under a year, between January and December 1936, and was never crowned. He became the first and only English monarch to abandon the throne voluntarily.

Many people in Britain were outraged; they thought a king should show a greater sense of loyalty to his people, and not place his own selfish interests above his duty to the nation. After Edward VIII abdicated he married Wallis Simpson. They became the Duke and Duchess of Windsor and went to live abroad, mainly in Paris, where he died in 1972.

roadcasting to the nation

t was George V, father of George VI, who made the first ever royal Christmas broadcast on the radio, in 1932. It established the radio as a means for the sovereign to talk directly to the nation – most people had never previously heard a monarch speak. Edward VIII used radio to broadcast his message about his abdication in December 1936. The coronation of George VI was broadcast on the radio in 1937; and in 1940, at the age of 14, Princess Elizabeth (the present Queen), accompanied by Princess Margaret, broadcast a message to the children of the British Empire.

George VI: 1936–1952

With Edward VIII gone, the job of being king fell to his younger brother 'Bertie', the Duke of York, who chose to be called George VI. He was a shy man, and suffered from a stammer, but he had a strong and confident wife, Lady Elizabeth Bowes-Lyon. They had two young daughters, Princess Elizabeth and Princess Margaret. The nation warmed to them – which was fortunate, because it needed steadfast and popular leaders to steer it through the next major crisis: the Second World War.

The Second World War
(1939-1945)

So it was war again, barely twenty years after the disastrous First World War – and with the same old enemy, Germany (this time led by the dictator Adolf Hitler), plus Italy and Japan. The King and Queen remained in London, lending vital support to the Prime Minister, Winston Churchill, and comforting the victims of war – visiting, for instance, badly bombed areas in the East End of London.

When bombs struck Buckingham Palace in 1940, the Queen said: 'I am glad we have been bombed. It makes me feel we can look the East End in the face.'

In 1945, aged 18, Princess Elizabeth joined the army, in the Auxiliary Transport Service (ATS). During the war the royal family earned the respect and affection of the nation for their quiet but steadfast work and support – restoring much of the loyalty that had been lost with the abdication of Edward VIII.

...abeth II: 1952–present

...incess Elizabeth was 25 years old when her father died of lung cancer, in February 1952. She was crowned in June 1953. By this time she had two children: Prince Charles (born 1948) and Princess Anne (born 1950). Prince Andrew was born in 1960, and Prince Edward in 1964. In 1947, on her 21st birthday, when on tour in Africa, she made a broadcast in which she said: 'I declare before you all that my whole life, whether it be long

Prince Philip

In 1947, Elizabeth married a handsome prince, Philip Mountbatten (born 1921), the son of Prince Andrew of Greece and Denmark. After attending school at Gordonstoun in Scotland, he joined the Royal Navy in 1938, and served throughout the Second World War. Following his engagement to Princess Elizabeth, he became Duke of Edinburgh. In 1956 he developed the Duke of Edinburgh Award scheme, to encourage life skills and community spirit among young people, and he has also been an active President of the World Wildlife Fund – while performing the delicate background role of Prince Consort to a Queen regnant.

or short, shall be devoted to your se~
Her life has been long, and she has been t~
to her word.

Coronation

The coronation of a monarch is one of the greatest ceremonial occasions in Britain. Because of the huge amount of organisation involved, it often takes place many months after the monarch actually inherits the throne. Queen Elizabeth II was crowned on 2 June 1953, over a year after her accession.

As this is a religious event, the actual crowning takes place in Westminster Abbey, on the throne of Edward I. The monarch takes a series of oaths and is anointed by holy oil, then is crowned and handed the royal regalia (the Crown Jewels). The event is attended by thousands of dignitaries from around the world, while the public can line the streets to watch the procession of the horse-drawn royal coaches and the military in their finest dress uniforms.

The Commonwealth of Nations

After the First World War, the term 'British Commonwealth' was used to acknowledge the status of Canada, Australia and other 'dominions' as independent but linked to Britain. After the Second World War, the old British Empire rapidly disintegrated, as British possessions such as India, Ghana, Jamaica, Malaya and Papua New Guinea were granted independence. As they became independent, most of them joined the Commonwealth. Now called the Commonwealth of Nations, it clubs together 54 countries, with Queen Elizabeth II as its head. It provides an arena in which to share and promote cultural activities and common values, such as human rights, the law, democracy and free trade.

The Queen remains the Head of State of 16 of the Commonwealth Realms: the United Kingdom, Canada, Australia, New Zealand, Jamaica, Barbados, the Bahamas, Grenada, Papua New Guinea, the Solomon Islands, Tuvalu, Saint Lucia, Saint Vincent and the Grenadines, Belize, Antigua and Barbuda, and Saint Kitts and Nevis. Some of these, notably Australia, periodically raise the question of whether they wish to become a republic and no longer have the Queen as Head of State – a question that is always hotly disputed, because the Queen still has loyal supporters in all her realms.

The Queen Mother

Elizabeth Bowes-Lyon (1900–2002), daughter of the 14th Earl of Strathmore and Kinghorne, was catapulted into the role of Queen when Edward VIII abdicated in 1936. When her daughter Elizabeth inherited the throne, she became known as Queen Elizabeth the Queen Mother. She remained in the public eye, attending public functions, and famously enjoying horse-racing. When she died aged 101 in 2002, more than 200,000 people filed past her coffin as she lay in state in Westminster Hall.

Princess Margaret

Queen Elizabeth's sister Margaret (1930–2002) was four years her junior, but remained a close companion throughout her life. Her happy and gilded youth was clouded in the 1950s when she was prevented from marrying the dashing pilot Group Captain Peter Townsend, because he was considered unsuitable as a divorced man. Instead, she married Antony Armstrong-Jones, a noted society photographer, who became Lord Snowdon. They had two children, but divorced in 1978. Margaret died aged 71 in 2002, seven weeks before her mother.

The Queen's children

Divorced, divorced, divorced... survived

Prince Charles, Prince of Wales

Born in 1948, the first child of Queen Elizabeth, Charles was formally crowned Prince of Wales in an elaborate investiture ceremony at Caernarfon Castle at the age of 20. In 1981 he married Lady Diana Spencer. They had two sons, William (born 1982) and Harry (properly Henry, born 1984), but the marriage foundered, and Charles and Diana separated in the late 1980s. Then, in 1997, Diana was killed in a car crash in Paris. In 2005, Prince Charles married his former girlfriend, Camilla Parker-Bowles, who took the title of Duchess of Cornwall. Charles remains highly committed to a broad variety of issues, helping the underprivileged through the Prince's Trust charity, and supporting organic farming and traditional architecture.

Princess Anne, the Princess Royal

Born in 1950, she married Captain Mark Phillips in 1984, but they divorced in 1992. Their children are Peter (born 1977) and Zara (born 1981). In 1992 she married Commander Timothy Laurence, an officer in the Royal Navy. Celebrated as a gifted horse-rider, she took part in the 1976 Olympic Games. As patron of some 200 organisations, and carrying out 700 public engagements every year, she is one of the hardest-working members of the royal family.

Prince Andrew, Duke of York
Born in 1960, he married Sarah Ferguso
1986; they were divorced in 1996. Their t,
daughters are Beatrice (born 1988) and
Eugenie (born 1990).

Prince Edward, Earl of Wessex
Born in 1964, he married Sophie Rhys-Jones in
1999; their children are Louise (born 2003)
and James (born 2007).

The order of succession

Succession in Britain goes through the male
line, in the first instance – a system called 'male
primogeniture'. If a monarch has sons and
daughters, the sons (and their offspring) take
precedence. The sons or daughters of the
monarch's eldest son take precedence over
the second son. A daughter will become queen
only if she has no living brothers, and there are
no children of a brother who has died.

1. Charles, Prince of Wales
2. Prince William of Wales
3. Prince Henry (Harry) of Wales
4. Prince Andrew, Duke of York
5. Princess Beatrice of York
6. Princess Eugenie of York
7. Prince Edward, Earl of Wessex
8. James, Viscount Severn
9. Lady Louise Windsor
10. Princess Anne, the Princess Royal

~narchy in the television age

George VI's coronation was the first ever to be broadcast on television – but that was in 1937, when televisions were rare. However, the coronation of Elizabeth II in 1953 was watched on television by some 20 million viewers. Every year on Christmas Day, the Queen broadcasts a television message to the nation, a tradition that she began with a live broadcast in 1957. Over the years, television has been used by the royal family to give a greater insight into their lives and work than has ever been available to the public before.

The jubilees

The 25th year of the Queen's reign was marked by the celebration of her Silver Jubilee in 1977. At the time, it was not clear that the British nation was sufficiently supportive of the monarchy to make much of the occasion. As it turned out, the nation erupted into street parties and parades. The Queen toured the UK extensively, and also visited a number of Commonwealth nations. The Golden Jubilee in 2002 marked 50 years in similar fashion.

Regal Beasts

Symbols of animals appear in many coats of arms, not least the Royal Coat of Arms, which features a lion and a unicorn. But animals don't just have a symbolic role to play in royal life.

Royal dogs: Valuable, pedigree dogs have always served as status symbols among European royalty, and the Kings and Queens of Britain were no exception. Richard II had greyhounds; the Scottish deerhound was the 'royal dog of Scotland', and at one time could be owned only by royalty; Charles II was fond of a breed now known as Cavalier King Charles Spaniels; Queen Victoria had a collie called Noble. And Queen Elizabeth II has always had Welsh corgis – usually several at a time.

Royal horses: The royal family has a close bond with horses. The Queen breeds racehorses at the Royal Stud near Sandringham, and, like her mother, is a keen follower of the sport. The Duke of Edinburgh is an expert in carriage-driving. Prince Charles and his sons play polo. Princess Anne has passed her horse-riding skills on to her daughter Zara Phillips, who is a leading figure in international three-day-eventing horse trials. Horses also play a major role in royal processions: coaches are drawn by teams of Windsor Greys and Bays, kept at Windsor and in the Royal Mews behind Buckingham Palace.

Buckingham Palace

This is the principal residence of the royal family in London – a place that serves both as a London home and a glittering setting for formal and ceremonial occasions. The original house was built in 1705 for the 1st Duke of Buckingham. It was bought in 1762 by George III, who enlarged it with the West Wing, overlooking the gardens. This wing contains the grand state apartments, including the Throne Room and the State Dining Room (for banquets), and a Picture Gallery with a fabulous collection of paintings. Victoria made Buckingham Palace her official London residence, when she moved here from St James's Palace in 1837, and in the 1840s added the East Front, overlooking the Mall. The Palace now has 600 rooms, including 52 bedrooms.

The balcony on the East Front is where the royal family appears before the crowds on major public occasions.

The Changing of the Guard is the ceremony in which soldiers (usually from the Household Division in their bearskin hats and scarlet tunics) parade and replace the guards who stand on duty in sentry boxes outside the East Front.

When the Queen is in residence, the royal standard flies from the flagpole above the central gate.

The gardens cover 40 acres (16 hectares). Each year some 20,000 distinguished people are invited to garden parties at Buckingham Palaces, attended by the Queen.

Other royal residences

- **St James's Palace.** Built for Henry VIII; now used mainly as offices and for functions.
- **Clarence House.** Built 1825–1827, beside St James's Palace. It was the home of Queen Elizabeth the Queen Mother until 2002, and now is the London residence of Prince Charles and his family.
- **Kensington Palace.** Built in 1689 for William and Mary, it now contains the apartments of various members of the royal family, as well as royal collections.
- **Windsor Castle** is an old Norman fortress west of London.
- **Balmoral Castle,** in the Highlands of Scotland, was built in the 1850s for Queen Victoria and Prince Albert.
- **Sandringham House,** in Norfolk, was built for Edward VII as a young man, in the 1850s.
- **The Palace of Holyroodhouse,** Edinburgh: the Queen's official residence in Scotland.
- **The Castle of Mey** (on the north coast of Scotland) was built in the 16th century and was formerly owned by Queen Elizabeth the Queen Mother.

What the Queen does

'Queen Elizabeth the Second, by the Grace of God, of Great Britain and Northern Ireland and of her other Realms and Territories, Queen, Head of the Commonwealth, Defender of the Faith' – so went her job description at her coronation in 1953. Britain has a constitutional monarchy, which is to say that the King or Queen is the Head of State, but has limited power: running the country is mainly carried out by the government and Parliament.

That said, after an election it is Queen who invites the leader of the largest political party in the House of Commons to form a government and to become Prime Minister. She also formally dissolves Parliament when an election is required. All Acts of Parliament have to receive the Royal Assent before they become law. The Prime Minister visits the Queen on a regular basis to discuss political and national matters. In her constitutional role, the Queen is assisted by the selected group of senior politicians who form her Privy Council.

As Head of State she is on the same level as heads of state of other countries – monarchs or presidents – and so represents the United Kingdom at the highest level in international state functions.

The Queen is also:

- **Commander-in-Chief of the Armed Forces**
- **Supreme Governor of the Church of England**
- **Head of the Commonwealth**

Her public duties involve a mixture of formal ceremonies amd pageantry that is enjoyed as a public spectacle. Official occasions include:

Trooping the Colour: The Queen takes the salute at the military parade on Horse Guards Parade in London to mark her 'official birthday' in June.

State Opening of Parliament: Each new session of Parliament (usually once a year, in November or December) begins with this ceremony, during which the Queen, in the full regalia of state, reads the 'Queen's Speech', written by the government and announcing the programme of legislation.

Cenotaph Ceremony of Remembrance: Each November, the Queen attends the ceremony at the war memorial in Whitehall, London, to commemorate the dead of the two World Wars and other later conflicts.

Investitures: The Queen bestows honours, formally awarding titles such as Sir or Dame, honours such as OBEs and MBEs, or conferring medals for military gallantry.

The Crown Jewels

The fabulously valuable Crown Jewels are kept in a highly secure vault in the Tower of London, where they can be viewed by the public – a tradition that dates back to the 17th century.

Most of the original Crown Jewels were destroyed after the execution of Charles I in 1649. A new set was made for the coronation of Charles II in 1660. The only items that predate that time are the Coronation Spoon and three swords. Various crowns, orbs and sceptres have been added to the collection over time, for instance for Mary II, who was crowned as Queen (not Queen consort) alongside William III.

Among the 'Coronation Regalia' on show today are:

Imperial State Crown. Made for the coronation of George VI in 1937, it has 5 rubies, 11 emeralds, 17 sapphires, 273 pearls and 2,868 diamonds. This includes various historic gems, such as the Stuart Sapphire, the Black Prince's Ruby and Queen Elizabeth I's Pearls.

St Edward's Crown is used for coronations; made for Charles II, it dates from 1661.

Crown of Queen Elizabeth the Queen Mother: This contains the famous Koh-i-Noor diamond.

Orb: made for the coronation of Charle
A hollow, jewel-encrusted golden ball, it
symbol of sovereign power, with a cross fc
Christianity.

Sceptre with the Cross: The head is set with
Cullinan I (the First Star of Africa), the
largest high-quality cut diamond in the world.

Stealing the Crown Jewels

The crown jewels were stolen during Edward
I's reign. In 1303, Richard of Pudlicott spent
three months digging a tunnel into the
Treasury of Westminster Abbey. He was later
arrested and hanged, then his flayed skin was
displayed on the Treasury door.

In 1671 'Colonel' Thomas Blood and
accomplices made a bold attempt to run off with
the crown, orb and sceptre, but were arrested
just outside the Tower of London. Blood was
generously pardoned by King Charles II.

Longest reigns: (1) Victoria: 63 years 216 days; (2) Elizabeth II: 59 years 96 days. (Elizabeth II has to reign until 10 September 2015 to beat Victoria.)

Shortest reigns: (1) Lady Jane Grey: 9 days; (2) Alfward: 16 days (924); (3) Edward IV (one of the Princes in the Tower): about 78 days.

Oldest monarch on accession: William IV, who was 64 when he became King. The next oldest was Edward VII (59).

Youngest monarch on accession: Mary, Queen of Scots: 6 days (but crowned at 9 months).

Tallest king: (1) Edward IV: 1.91 m (6 ft 3 in); (2) Henry VIII: 1.88 m (6 ft 2 in – about the same as Prince William, Duke of Cambridge).

Last English king to die in battle: Richard III, at the battle of Bosworth Field, 1485.

Last British king to die in battle: James IV of Scotland, at the Battle of Flodden, 1513.

Last king to lead his troops into battle: George II (Battle of Dettingen, 1743).

Youngest marriage: In 1328 the future David II of Scotland, aged 4, married Joan, the daughter of Edward II, aged 7.

Most legitimate children: George III: 15.

Most illegitimate children: (1) Henry I: 20–25, with 6 mothers, allegedly; (2) Charles II: he acknowledged 14, with eight mothers; (3) William IV: 10 with Dorothea Bland ('Mrs Jordan').

Willy Willy Harry Steve

A rhyme to help you remember the Kings and Queens of England:

Willy, Willy, Harry, Steve,
Henry, Dick, John, Henry three;
Then three Edwards, Richard two,
Henry four, five, six, then who?
Edward four, five, Dick the bad,
Two more Henries, Ned the lad;
Bloody Mary she came next,
Then we have our Good Queen Bess.
From Scotland we got James the Vain;
Charlie one, two, James again.
William and Mary, Anna Gloria,
Four Georges, William and Victoria.
Edward, George, the same again,
Now Elizabeth – and the end.

Glossary

abdication Giving up the throne voluntarily.

accession The moment when a new king or queen takes power (the coronation may follow later).

Alba The Scottish Gaelic word for Scotland.

anoint To pour holy oil on the head (and hands and heart) of the sovereign, as part of the coronation ceremony.

coronation The ceremony of crowning a new king or queen.

crown The ornamental headdress worn by a king or queen to demonstrate their status; by extension, the word Crown is used to refer to the sovereign, and the sovereign's authority.

dynastic marriage An arranged marriage, usually between princes and princesses of different nations, designed to reinforce diplomatic or territorial connections between ruling families.

HRH His or Her Royal Highness, a style of address used for princes and princesses in the British royal family.

Majesty a term used to refer to the sovereign. Derived from the Latin *maiestas*, meaning 'greatness', it was first adopted in Britain by Henry VIII.

monarch A king or queen (or emperor or empress); derived from Greek *mono* ('single') + *arkhes* ('ruler').

orb A golden sphere, surmounted by a cross, part of the Crown Jewels. It symbolises the power of the sovereign.

primogeniture The system of inheritance that favours the firstborn; succession in the British monarchy follows male primogeniture (the eldest son inherits).

Prince Consort The husband of a queen, where the queen has inherited the throne in her own right ('Queen Regnant').

Princess Royal The title traditionally given to the British monarch's eldest daughter. Held for life, the title is only conferred when an existing Princess Royal dies.

Queen Consort The wife of a reigning king who is not queen in her own right.

Queen Regnant A queen who has inherited the throne and rules in her own right, not through marriage to a king.

Regent Someone who rules on behalf of the king or queen (for instance, when a king is too ill to rule for himself).

Royal Warrant An official acknowledgement awarded by senior members of the royal family to selected suppliers of goods or services.

sceptre A ceremonial golden rod, part of the Crown Jewels. It symbolises the authority of the sovereign.

succession The right of inheritance that hands the role of king or queen to the next in line.

...ings & queens timeline

AD 43–c.450 The Romans occupy Britain.

c.400–500 Germanic tribes, such as the Anglo-Saxons, settle in England.

793 The Vikings attack Lindisfarne, in their first major raid on Britain.

802–839 Reign of Egbert, first of the SAXON dynasty of kings.

842 Kenneth MacAlpin is crowned king of the Picts and Scots at Scone.

871–899 Reign of Alfred the Great, who unites the English to face the Viking invaders.

1016 Canute of Denmark becomes king of England.

1040 Macbeth defeats Duncan I to become King of Alba (Scotland).

1042 Edward the Confessor starts building Westminster Abbey.

1066 The NORMANS, led by William the Conqueror, win the Battle of Hastings.

1078 Work begins on the Tower of London.

1096–1099 The First Crusade is launched to win Christian control of the Holy Land.

1154 Henry II becomes the first PLANTAGENET king.

1155 The English Pope Adrian IV hands Ireland to Henry II.

1215 King John is forced to sign Magna Carta.

1272–1307 Reign of Edward I.

1290 Death of Margaret, the 'Maid of Norway', infant queen of Scotland.

1296 Edward I invades Scotland and seizes the Stone of Destiny (Stone of Scone).

1297 William Wallace defeats the English at Stirling Bridge.

1305 Robert the Bruce becomes King of Scotland.

1314 The Scots defeat Edward II at Bannockburn.

1348–1350 The Black Death kills one third of the British population.

1371–1390 Reign of Robert II, first STEWART king of Scotland.

1399 Henry IV becomes the first king of the House of LANCASTER.

1415 Henry V defeats the French at the Battle of Agincourt.

1455–1485 The Wars of the Roses.

1461 Edward IV becomes the first king of the House of YORK.

1485 Richard III is defeated and killed at the Battle of Bosworth Field; Henry VII becomes the first TUDOR king.

1492 Christopher Columbus, sponsored by the king of Spain, reaches the Americas.

1547 Reign of Henry VIII.

The German priest Martin Luther begins his protest against the Roman Catholic Church.

1533 Henry VIII divorces his first wife Catherine of Aragon, resulting in the break with the Roman Catholic Church.

1555 The persecution of Protestants begins in England, two years into the reign of Mary I.

1558–1603 Reign of Elizabeth I.

1584 Sir Walter Raleigh begins the colonisation of Virginia.

1587 Execution of Mary, Queen of Scots on the orders of Elizabeth I.

1588 The Spanish Armada is defeated.

1603 In the 'Union of Crowns', James VI of Scotland becomes James I of England, the first STUART king of England.

1605 The Gunpowder Plot is discovered in the Houses of Parliament.

1618–1648 Continental Europe is plunged into the destructive and bloody Thirty Years' War.

1620 The Pilgrim Fathers sail to North America in the *Mayflower*. They found the Plymouth colony.

1643–1715 Reign of Louis XIV of France.

1649 Charles I is executed during the English Civil War. Britain will have no monarch for 11 years.

1660 Monarchy resumes with the Restoration of Charles II.

1665–1666 The Great Plague of London is followed by the Great Fire of London.

1688 James II is ejected as William and Mary take over the throne following the 'Glorious Revolution'.

1698 Fire destroys most of the royal Palace of Whitehall in London.

1701 Act of Union: Scotland joins England and Wales in a United Kingdom, with the same monarch and parliament.

1714 George I becomes the first HANOVERIAN king.

1715 First Jacobite Rebellion against England, led by the Old Pretender.

1745–1746 Last Jacobite Rebellion ends in defeat at Culloden.

1775–1783 American War of Independence.

1789 The French Revolution removes Louis XVI from the throne.

1799 Napoleon Bonaparte takes control of France.

1801 The Act of Union unites Great Britain and Ireland.

Admiral Nelson dies achieving a great English victory at the Battle of Trafalgar.

1811 As George III slides into mental illness, his son George takes over as Prince Regent.

1815 Napoleon defeated at Waterloo.

1834 The Houses of Parliament at Westminster are destroyed by fire.

1837–1901 Reign of Victoria.

1848 Revolutions break out across Europe (France, Germany, Austria, Italy, Hungary).

1861 Prince Albert dies, aged 42.

1865 US President Abraham Lincoln is assassinated.

1897 Victoria celebrates her Diamond Jubilee, marking the 60th year of her reign.

1901 Edward VII becomes the first king of the House of SAXE-COBURG-GOTHA.

1914–1918 First World War.

1917 The Royal Family changes its name to the House of WINDSOR to distance itself from its German origins.

1922 Ireland (apart from Northern Ireland) becomes independent from Britain.

1932 George VI broadcasts the first Christmas message to the nation by radio.

1936 Abdication of Edward VIII.

1939–1945 Second World War; it ends with the first and only military use of atomic bombs, dropped on the Japanese cities of Hiroshima and Nagasaki.

1947 India and Pakistan become independent, as Britain begins to dismant its empire.

1952 Queen Elizabeth II accedes to the throne.

1953 News of the first conquest of Mount Everest coincides with the coronation of Elizabeth II.

2002 Elizabeth II celebrates her Golden Jubilee, marking the 50th year of her reign.

2011 Prince William, Duke of Cambridge marries Catherine Middleton at Westminster Abbey.

2012 Year of Elizabeth II's Diamond Jubilee, marking the 60th year of her reign.

2013 The birth of Prince George of Cambridge, the son of Prince William, Duke of Cambridge, and Catherine, Duchess of Cambridge.

Index

Key to cover picture

Top row, L–R: Elizabeth I, Alfred the
Great, Elizabeth II, Henry V, Victoria
Centre: Henry VIII
Bottom row, L–R: James I & VI, Mary
Queen of Scots, Charles I, George IV

H.M. KING GEORGE V
IN IMPERIAL ROBES